THE GREAT CONTRIBUTION TO WORLD PEACE AND SOCIAL HARMONY OF EMPEROR ASHOKA AND EMPEROR TRẦN NHÂN TÔNG

SỰ ĐÓNG GÓP CHO HÒA BÌNH THẾ GIỚI VÀ AN TOÀN XÃ HỘI CỦA HOÀNG ĐẾ A-DỤC VÀ VUA TRẦN NHÂN TÔNG

Ni sư Tiến sĩ T.N. Giới Hương

Bảo Anh Lạc Bookshelf 101

THE GREAT CONTRIBUTION TO WORLD PEACE AND SOCIAL HARMONY OF EMPEROR ASHOKA AND EMPEROR TRẦN NHÂN TÔNG

SỰ ĐÓNG GÓP CHO HÒA BÌNH THẾ GIỚI VÀ AN TOÀN XÃ HỘI CỦA HOÀNG ĐẾ A-DỤC VÀ VUA TRẦN NHÂN TÔNG

Song ngữ Anh - Việt

Ven. Dr. Bhikṣuṇī Thich Nu Gioi Huong

Ton Giao Publishing

Huong Sen Buddhist Temple

19865 Seaton Avenue, Perris, CA 92570, USA

Tel: 951-657-7272, Cell: 951-616- 8620

Email: huongsentemple@gmail.com,

thichnugioihuong@yahoo.com

Facebook: https://www.facebook.com/ huongsentemple

Web: www.huongsentemple.com

MỤC LỤC

THE GREAT CONTRIBUTION TO WORLD PEACE AND SOCIAL HARMONY OF EMPEROR ASHOKA AND EMPEROR TRẦN NHÂN TÔNG

Buddhist Seminar at Siddharth United Social Welfare Mission, Chinar Park, Kolkata, India, July 2 2023

Presented by Ven. Dr. Bhikṣuṇī T.N. Gioi Huong

To begin with, it seems it is proper and appropriate to jot down a few sentences on the Buddha, Buddhism, and religious background of India and

Vietnam before coming to the subject of concern, "The Great Contribution to World Peace and Social Harmony of Emperor Ashoka of India and Emperor Trần Nhân Tông of Vietnam."

India and Vietnam maintain centuries-old traditional relations, particularly in the field of culture along with other political, trade, and economic affiliations. Both countries equally respect and honor each other's religious and national leaders.

I. THE SAKYAMUNI BUDDHA IN INDIA

During several centuries before the Christian Era, the civilized part of India was divided into sixteen realms, eight of which were kingdoms, and t he remaining were republics. Among those kingdoms the most powerful were Magadha and Kosala.

Indian map (Google)[1]

The little Sakya republic was ruled by the king of Kosala who received tribute. The Sakyas were of the Kshatriya Solar Dynasty and were called the "eslverajas" or "kings."[2] In the middle of the century, their chief was King Suddhodana who had his capital at Kapilawastu. In the year 623 BC his queen, Maha Maya, was traveling from Kapilavastu to her parent's home in Devdaha to have her first child. On her way the queen gave birth to a divine son in the Lumbini grove between two tall Sal trees.

An old sage named Asita visited King Suddhodana and predicted the royal baby would one day become the savior of human beings. The royal baby was named Siddhartha. The king provided all protection and gave him every comfort. When Siddhartha was young, his father, Suddhodana, arranged for him to marry a beautiful princess named Yasodhara. They had one child, a son named Rahula. Even before the marriage, Prince Siddhartha had a strong desire to leave the worldly life, which his father prevented. After the birth of his son, Siddhartha thought his son would be an obstacle to his future steps. One day he decided to leave the worldly life and accordingly, while his wife and son were sleeping, he left the palace without anyone noticing.

In his chariot he rode away passing through a forest. He discarded his royal robes, cut his long hair with his sword and became an ascetic. He went in search of teachers who could teach him the truth of life. He imbibed all that they had to teach him, but his thirst for truth remained unanswered and unquenched. He moved on and ultimately reached a picturesque land at a place presently known as Bodh Gaya. In accordance with the belief that

---

1. 1. https://www.buddhisttour.com/map.html

2. Bapat, P.V. 2500 Years of Buddhism. Department of Information, Government of India, New Delhi, 1959, 1–7.

the mind became elevated by emancipating the body, he practiced rigid austerities and resorted to different kinds of self-torture for six years. He lived in this manner and was reduced to a skeleton. At this stage he realized that physical torture was not the way to achieve enlightenment and decided to partake of food again.

Gotama Bodhisatta meditating on the Nairanjana River

After consuming a bowl of milk rice offered to him by the young girl, Sujata, daughter of a wealthy merchant, he regained good health. After several attempts to control and set the mind free, he attained enlightenment under a Bodhi tree, now known as Sri Maha Bodhi. With this, a human being was able to "experience and understand how to escape from suffering and teach others."[3] In the history of Indian religions, Buddhism occupies a unique place, firstly for throwing its portals open not only to Indians, but to all sections of the world society. From the beginning, Buddhism has always been based on "peace, tolerance, nonviolence, and solidarity as a world religion."[4]

3. Mahajan, V.D. Chand and Co. Ancient India. Ram Nagar: New Delhi, 295–298.

4. Dharmapal, Maha Thera. Ashoka – 2300. India: The Bengal Buddhist

II. EMPERORS AND KINGS OF THE BUDDHA'S PERIOD

During the lifetime of Sakyamuni Buddha, he received royal patronage from powerful kings and queens.

King Bimbisara of Magadha was the first to offer him a temple for residence. Bimbisara's queen, Khema, became an ardent Buddhist. After the Buddha's demise, Ajasatta, son of King Bimbisara, organized the first Buddhist conference or "sangayana" at Rajgir.[5] King Prasanjith Kosala of Sravasti (modern-day Uttar Pradesh) was a patron of Buddhism. It was at Sravasti that the Buddha spent most of the rainy seasons (Vassana).The Lichchavis of the Republic of Lichchavis (present-day Bihar) were followers of the Buddha and he reorganized their seven non-depending laws to be included in the Buddhist order.

In Kosambi under the rule of King Udeni, the first conflict among bhikkus occurred. They divided into two divisions-Dhamma and Vinaya.

No one can forget king Suddhodana of Kapilawattu, father of the Buddha. He paid maximum respect and veneration to Buddha. Besides Emperor Ashoka, there were other great rulers who patronized the Buddha and Buddhism in different ways. They enriched and propagated Buddhism in different parts of the world: King Dharmaraj Milinda (circa 175 BC), Emperor Kanishka (78– 101 or 120 AD), and Emperor Harshawardhana (425 AD) are a few of them.

King Ansuverma of Nepal (seventh century AD), Emperor Tsrong Tsang Gampo of Tibet (617 AD), Emperor Yu Tee of Liang Dynasty China (502–549 AD), King Wang Kiyen of Korea (1340 AD), Shoroku, known

5. Association, Kolkata. 1997. 15, 121, 178. Medhankara, Ven. Dr. Maha Thero. The Great Buddhist Emperors of Asia. Bhoomi Prakashan. Nagpur, Maharashrtra, India, 1959. 1, 41, 56, 72, 93, 100, 110, 128, 134, 146, 169, 195, 222, 234, 246, 272.

as the Japanese Dharmashoka (580 AD), Dhamma Cheti of Burma (1476 AD), Emperor Dutugamunu of Sri Lanka (101–77 BC), Maha Parakramabahu of Sri Lanka (1153–1186), Emperor Kublai Khan of Mongolia (1254 AD), Sri Suryawansam of Siam (Thailand; 1355 AD), Jayaverma of Cambodia (1182–1202 AD), King Fanewn of Laos (1353 AD), King Indra Verma II of the Champa Kingdom, present-day Vietnam (860–890 AD), and Sri Vijayaag were other rulers who spread Buddhism in the above-mentioned countries.[6]

II. ASHOKA EMPEROR

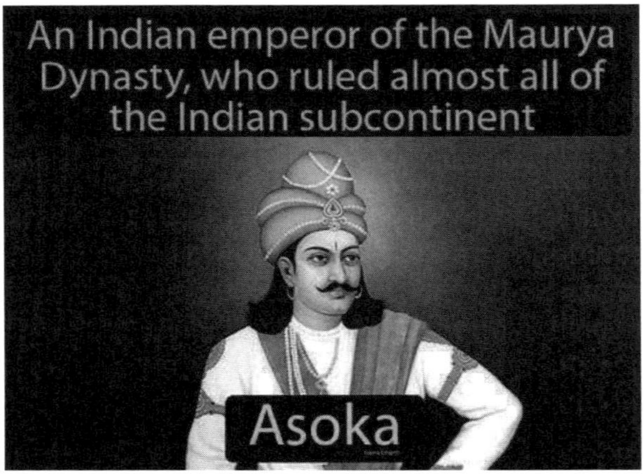

Ashoka, an Indian emperor of the Maurya Dynasty who ruled almost all of the Indian subcontinent from c. 268 to 232 BC, was one of India's greatest emperors. Ashoka reigned over a realm that stretched from the Hindu Kush Mountains in Afghanistan to the modern state of Bangladesh in the east. It covered the entire Indian subcontinent except parts of present-day Tamil Nadu and Kerala. The empire's capital was Pataliputra (in Magadha, present-day Bihar),

6. Bapat, P.V. 2500 Years of Buddhism. India: Bapat Ministry of Information and Broadcasting, Government of India, 1959. 50, 53, 56.

with provincial capitals at Taxila and Ujjain.

Around 260 BCE, Ashoka waged a bitterly destructive war against the state of Kalinga (modern Orissa). He conquered Kalinga, which none of his ancestors had done. He embraced Buddhism after wiT.N.essing the mass deaths of the Kalinga War, which he himself had waged out of a desire for conquest. Ashoka reflected on the war in Kalinga, which reportedly had resulted in more than 100,000 deaths and 150,000 deportations, ending at around 200,000 deaths. Ashoka converted gradually to Buddhism beginning about 263 BCE He was later dedicated to the propagation of Buddhism across Asia, and established monuments marking several significant sites in the life of Gautama Buddha. Ashoka regarded Buddhism as a doctrine that could serve as a cultural foundation for political unity. Ashoka is now remembered as a philanthropic administrator. In the Kalinga edicts, he addresses his people as his "children," and mentions that as a father, he desires their good.

"Aśoka" means "painless, without sorrow" in Sanskrit. In his edicts, he is referred to as Devānāmpriya (Pali: Devānaṃpiya or "Beloved of the Gods"), and Priyadarśin (Pali: Piyadasī or "He who regards everyone with affection"). His fondness for his name's connection to the Saraca asoca tree, or the "Ashoka Tree"[7] is also referenced in the Ashokavadana.

H.G. Wells wrote of Ashoka in his book, The Outline of History:[8] "Amidst the tens of thousands of names of monarchs that crowd the columns of history, their majesties and graciousnesses and serenities and royal highnesses and the like, the name of Ashoka shines and shines, almost alone, a star." Along with the Edicts of Ashoka, his

7. Bhandarakar, D.R. Aśoka, Calcutta: Calcutta University Press, 1969. 166, 230.

8. H.G. Wells (1866–1946). A Short History of the World. 1922.

legend is related to the second century CE Ashokavadana ("Narrative of Ashoka," a part of the Divyavadana), and in the Sri Lankan text, Mahavamsa (Great Chronicle). The emblem of the modern Republic of India is an adaptation of the Lion Capital of Ashoka. The Dhammachakka or the wheel of Dhamma is depicted in India's national flag.

3.1. Ashoka's Early Life

Ashoka was born to the Mauryan emperor, Bindusara, and his wife, Dharmā (or Dhamma). He was the grandson of Chandragupta Maurya, founder of the Mauryan Dynasty. The Avadana texts mention that his mother was queen Subhadrangī. According to the Ashokavadana, she was the daughter of a Brahmin from the city of Champa.

3.2. Conquest of Kalinga

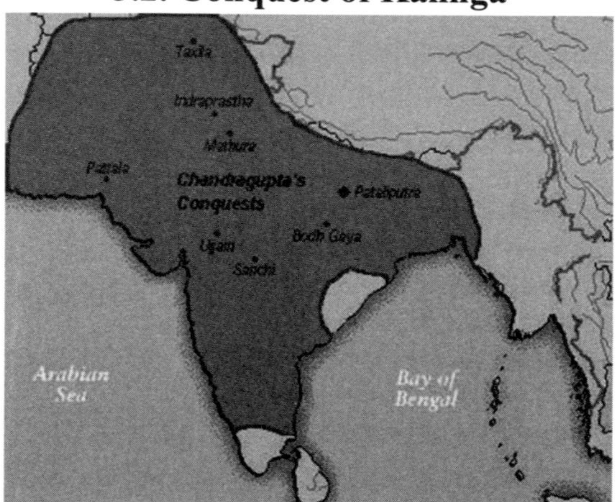

Kalinga (adjacent to the Bay of Bengal) and the Maurya Empire (blue) before the attack of Ashoka the Great

Ashoka's fighting qualities were apparent from an early age, and he was given royal military training. Because of his reputation as a frightening warrior and a heartless general, he was sent to curb "the riots in the Avanti province of the Mauryan empire."[9] The Buddhist text, Divyavadana, describes Ashoka putting down a revolt due to activities of wicked ministers. This may have been an incident in Bindusara's times. Taranatha's account states that Chanakya, Bindusara's chief advisor, destroyed the nobles and kings of sixteen towns and made himself the master of all territory between the eastern and the western seas. Some historians consider this an indication of Bindusara's conquest of the Deccan, while others consider it a suppression of a revolt. Following this, Ashoka was stationed at Ujjayini as governor. Bindusara's death in 272 BC led to a war over succession. Ascending to the throne, Ashoka expanded his empire over the next eight years.

While the early part of Ashoka's reign was apparently quite bloodthirsty, he became a follower of the Buddha's teachings after his conquest of Kalinga on the east coast of India in the present- day states of Orissa and North Coastal Andhra Pradesh. Kalinga was a state that prided itself on its sovereignty and democracy.

---

9. Bongard-Levin, G.M. Mauryan India. India: Stosius, 1986. 136.

With its monarchical parliamentary democracy, it was quite an exception in ancient Bharata where there existed the concept of "Rajdharma" or "the duty of the rulers," which was intrinsically entwined with the concept of bravery and dharma. The Kalinga War happened eight years after Ashoka's coronation. From his thirteenth inscription, we know that the battle was a massive one and caused the deaths of more than 100,000 soldiers and many civilians who rose up in defense; over 150,000 were deported. When he was walking through the grounds of Kalinga after his conquest, "rejoicing in his victory, he was moved by the number of bodies strewn there and the wails of the bereaved."[10]

3.3. Buddhist Conversion

His Majesty felt remorse at the conquest of Kalinga because during the subjugation of this previously unconquered country, slaughter, death, and kidnapping occurred, and His Majesty felt profound sorrow and regret. The edict goes on to address the even greater degree of sorrow and regret resulting from Ashoka's understanding that the friends and families of deceased would suffer greatly too. Legend says that one day after the war was

10. Aher, D.C. Ashoka the Great. Delhi: B.R. Publishers, 1995. 226, 228. https://en.wikipedia.org/wiki/Kalinga_War

over, Ashoka ventured out to roam the city and all he could see were burnt houses and scattered corpses.

The lethal war with Kalinga transformed the vengeful Emperor Ashoka to a stable and peaceful emperor and he became a patron of Buddhism. According to the prominent Indologist, A. L. Basham, Ashoka's personal religion became Buddhism, if not before, then certainly after the Kalinga war. However, according to Basham, the Dharma officially propagated by Ashoka was not Buddhism at all. Nevertheless, his patronage led to the expansion of Buddhism in the Mauryan empire and other kingdoms during his rule and worldwide from about 250 BCE.

Prominent in this cause were his son Mahinda (Mahendra) and daughter Sanghamitra (whose name means "friend of the Sangha"), who established Buddhism in Ceylon (now Sri Lanka). Information about the life and reign of Ashoka primarily comes from a relatively small number of Buddhist sources. In particular, the Sanskrit Ashokavadana (Story of Ashoka), written in the second century, and the two Pāli chronicles of Sri Lanka (the Dipavamsa and Mahavamsa), provide most of the currently known information about Ashoka. Additional information is contributed by the Edicts of Ashoka, whose authorship was finally attributed to the Ashoka of Buddhist legend after the discovery of dynastic lists that gave the name used in the edicts (Priyadarshi, "He who regards everyone with affection") as a title or additional name of Ashoka Maurya. Architectural remains of his period have been found at "Kumhrar, PaT.N.a, which include an eighty-pillar hypostyle hall."[11]

King Asoka truely confessed and ceased digvijaya (conquest by war) and sought for dhammavijaya (conquest by Dhamma). He ruled his country by Buddha-Dharma with numerous good deeds. His reign became more humane as he ruled according to the Dhamma. He was the first king to build major edicts with Buddhist inscriptions all over India and Central Asia. He set up a department of religious officers to look into moral education for the people. He went on dhammayatra (pilgrimages) to the holy places. He was generous with the requisites for the Sangha and supported them handsomely. He claimed to his neighbours that he had no expansionist intentions towards countries bordering his empire. After the Third Buddhist Council, missionary work to the adjacent nine countries saw the spread of Theravada Buddhism under his patronage. The nine countries are Kashmir and Gandhara (N. Punjab), Mahisamandala (South of Vindhyan mountains), Vanavasi (N. Kanara), Aparantaka (N. Gujarat, Kathiawar, Kacch and Sind), Maharattha (country of the Marathi, modern Bombay), Yona countries (clans of foreign race on NW frontier, Greeco-Bactrian kingdom), Himavanta (Himalayan region), Suvannabhumi (Lower Myanmar, Thailand, Java, and even Malaya) and Tambapanni (Sri Lanka) and so on.[12]

Ashoka spent lots of wealth for religious education, building monasteries and monuments. He also built

11. Ayyar, Sulochana. Costume and Ornaments as Depicted in the Early Sculptures of Gwarlior Museum. 186.

12. http://www.suttas.com/king-asoka.html

the great stupa of Sanchi. He erected several thousand Buddhist monuments to enshrine the Buddha's relics. He built viharas for the monks and the famous vihara in Pataliputra was named after him, Asokarama. He also helped to develop viharas (intellectual hubs) such as Nalanda and Taxila in addition to constructing Sanchi and Mahabodhi Temple. He was the great support for the cause of the Triple Gem.

3.4. King Ashoka was the first person to worship Buddha's relics

Emperor Ashoka was one of among the first Indian Buddhist worshipers and was instrumental in leaving traces of ancient Buddhism to this day through construction works, inscriptions, pillars, monasteries, stupas, and so on.

In the 20th year of his reign, King Ashoka requested Master Buddhist Upagupta[13] to take him to visit all the Buddha sites in India. King Ashoka along with Maurya royal family under the guidance of Master Upagupta made this worship trip within 265 days to visit and worship all the holy relics in India, from Lam Bhikkhuni to Kushinagar, at each relic King Ashoka built stupas, stone stele and stone pillars to mark the place where the Buddha once stayed and preached while still alive. It is thanks to these stone pillars and stele that today Buddhist disciples know exactly about the Buddha's relics.[14]

Edicts of Ashoka

The Edicts of Ashoka are a collection of thirty-

13. Ưu ba cúc đa có nghĩa là: Upagupta (P), (S, P), Moggaliputta-Tissa (P) the fourth Patriarch, one of the 28 Buddhist Patriarchs in India. https://phatgiao.org.vn/tu-dien-phat-hoc-online/uu-ba-cuc-da-k18682. html

14. Tarthang Tulku (1994), Holy Places of the Buddha, Crytal Mirror, Volume Nine, Dharma Press, USA.

three inscriptions on the Pillars of Ashoka, as well as on boulders and cave walls, made by Ashoka during his reign. These inscriptions are dispersed throughout modern-day Pakistan and India and represent the first tangible evidence of Buddhism. The edicts describe in detail the first wide expansion of Buddhism through the sponsorship of one of the most powerful kings of Indian history, offering more information about "Ashoka's proselytism, moral precepts, religious precepts, and his notions of social and animal welfare."[15]

His pronouncements were written on rocks in the periphery of his kingdom, while pillars were erected along the main roads, and where pilgrims gather. Asoka's edicts were written in his own words. Asoka's edicts were found in more than thirty places throughout India, Nepal, Pakistan, and Afghanistan. Most of them were written in the native language of the place.

Asoka was engaged in spreading Buddhism through the rock, stone and pillar edicts erected in his empire and beyond. The Bhabru inscription called upon his people to respect and have faith in Buddha, Dhamma and Sangha. The individual morality that Asoka hoped to foster included respect towards parents, elders, teachers, friends, servants, ascetics and Brahmins. Girnar Rock Edict Three stressed filial duties.

He also encouraged generosity (dana), harmlessness towards life (avihimsa bhutanam), moderation in spending and saving, treating others properly and to be well learned in others' religions. The qualities of heart that are recommended by Asoka in the edicts indicate his deep spirituality. They include kindness, self- examination, truthfulness, gratitude, purity of heart, enthusiasm, loyalty, self- control and love of Dhamma. The following seven

15. Gokhale, Balkrishna Govind. Ashoka Maurya. USA: Irvington Publishers, 1966. 223, 228, 231.

Buddhist texts were encouraged for both sangha and lay disciples. These texts favoured by Asoka appeared to bear on the life of the monks, and the ethical standards to which Asoka was devoted. Asoka did not concern himself with the philosophy of Buddhism but with the ethical and practical application.

Munigatha is praised as the recluse who goes alone to find calm, annihilating further existences, strong in understanding, virtue and concentration. The Mauneya Sutta praises the calm and detachment of recluseship. The Rahulovada Sutta is where Buddha admonishes Rahula against conscious false speech. Upatissapasine is where Sariputta asked many questions.[16]

3.5. Ashoka-vadana Text (the Legend of Ashoka)

Ashoka Pillar in Lumbini
(the birthplace of Buddha), Nepal

The Ashoka-vadana is a second-century CE text related to the legend of Ashoka. The legend was translated into

16. http://www.suttas.com/king-asoka.html

Chinese by Fa Hien in 300 CE. It is essentially a Hinayana text, and its world is that of Mathura and northwest India. The emphasis of this little- known text is on exploring the relationship between the king and the community of monks (the Sangha) and setting up an ideal of religious life for the laity (the common person) by telling appealing stories about religious exploits. Emperor Ashoka used his state power to spread Buddhism strongly and effectively.

3.6. Animal Welfare

Ashoka's rock edicts declare that injuring living things is not good, and no animal should be sacrificed for slaughter. However, he did not prohibit common cattle slaughter or beef eating.

The reign of Ashoka Maurya might have disappeared into history as the ages passed by, had he not left behind records of his reign. These records are in the form of sculpted pillars and rocks inscribed with a variety of actions and teachings he wished to be published under his name. The language used for inscription was in one of the Prakrit "common" languages etched in a Brahmi script.

King Ashoka, the third monarch of the Indian Mauryan dynasty, is also considered as "one of the most exemplary rulers who ever lived."[17]

3.7. Buddhist Kingship

One of the more enduring legacies of Ashoka Maurya was the model that he provided for the relationship between Buddhism and the state. Throughout Theravada southeastern Asia, the model of rulership embodied by Ashoka replaced the notion of divine kingship that had

17. Nikam, N.A. and McKeon Richard. The Edicts of Ashoka. Chicago: Chicago University Press, 1959. 47, 52.

previously dominated (in the Angkor Kingdom, for instance). Under this model of "Buddhist kingship," the king sought to legitimize his rule not through descent from a divine source, but by supporting and earning the approval of the Buddhist Sangha.

Following Ashoka's example, kings established monasteries, funded the construction of stupas, and supported the ordination of monks in their kingdom. Many rulers also took an active role in resolving disputes over the status and regulation of the sangha, as Ashoka had when he called a conclave to settle a number of contentious issues during his reign. This development ultimately led to a close association in many Southeast Asian countries between the monarchy and the religious hierarchy, an association that can still be seen today in the state-supported Buddhism of Thailand and the traditional role of the Thai king as both a religious and secular leader. Ashoka also said that all his courtiers always governed the people in a moral manner.

3.8. Historical Archaeological Sources on Ashoka

Ashoka and other Buddhist figures were almost forgotten by the historians of early British India, but James Prinsep contributed to the revelation of historical sources. Another important historian was British archaeologist John Hubert Marshall, who was Director-General of the Archaeological Survey of India. His main interests were Sanchi and Sarnath, in addition to Harappa and Mohenjodaro. Sir Alexander Cunningham, a British archaeologist and army engineer, and often known as the father of the Archaeological Survey of India, unveiled heritage sites like the Bharhut Stupa, Sarnath, Sanchi, and the Mahabodhi Temple. Mortimer Wheeler, a British archaeologist, also exposed Ashokan historical sources, especially the Taxila.

The inscriptions of Ashoka's edicts

Bilingual inscriptions (in Greek and Aramaic) by King Ashoka were discovered at Kandahar (National Museum of Afghanistan).

He imposed a ban on killing of "all four-footed creatures that are neither useful nor edible," and of specific animal species including several birds, and certain types of fish and bulls, among others. He also banned the killing of female goats, sheep and pigs that were nursing their young; as well as up to the age of six months. He also "banned killing of all fish and castration of animals during certain periods such as Chaturmasa and Uposatha."[18]

Ashoka also abolished the royal hunting of animals

18. Dharmapal, Maha Thera. Ashoka–2300. Kolkata, India: The Bengal

and restricted the slaying of animals for food in the royal residence. Because he banned hunting, created many veterinary clinics, and eliminated meat eating on many holidays, the Mauryan Empire under Ashoka has been described as one of the very few instances in world history of a government treating its animals as citizens who are as deserving of its protection as the human residents. It means human right and animal right are as the same relatively.

3.9. Pillars of Ashoka (Ashokastambha)

King Asoka received many relics of the Buddha, so he built many stupas throughout the kingdom to worship as well as build pagodas and stupas to support the Triple Gem (Buddha-Dharma-Sangha).

Archaeologists excavated and found scattered finds across India as well as in the countries of Nepal, Pakistan and Afghanistan. These stone pillars are exquisitely sculpted and full of art. This is the earliest contribution of the Indus valley civilization, an ancient language of Harrapa, older than the ancient Sanskrit language, the language often found in stone pillars, today called Prakrita.

The earliest translations from stone pillars and steles show us the efforts of a powerful monarch to build a country based on Buddhist ethics with a policy of peace for the people. rising above all the diseases of greed, anger and ignorance of human life like a pillar that reads: "If the people, after hearing the Buddha's teachings, practice them, they will gain benefits in the Dharma."[19]

Buddhist Association, 1997. 70, 72.

19. John S. Strong: The Legend of King Ashoka (Princeton University Press), 1983.

Ashoka Pillar in Lumbini (the birthplace of Buddha), Nepal

The King advised people to practice "not killing, honoring parents and elders, respecting teachers, respectfully making offerings to Samanas and Brahmans, behaving well with relatives, and sharing." with friends, treat employees and servants with kindness, help the elderly, the poor, and the suffering."[20] In addition, in another inscription, King Ashoka had the Mahamangala Sutta engraved, this is a sutra that Buddha taught about the moral life of lay Buddhists. If applied correctly, happiness will be achieved. Happiness will come to them right in this present life as below:

"Many deities and men, yearning after good, have pondered on blessings. Pray, tell me the greatest

20. Lược theo bản Việt dịch của HT Thích Thiện Châu. Đại đế A-dục, Một ông vua hộ trì phật pháp. Thích Nguyên Tạng. 09/09/2015. https://thuvienhoasen.org/a23735/dai-de-a-duc-mot-ong-vua-ho-tri-phat-phap

blessing!"

"Not to associate with the foolish, but to associate with the wise; and to honour those who are worthy of honour.

To reside in a suitable locality, to have done meritorious actions in the past and to set oneself in the right course.

To have much learning, to be skillful in handicraft, well-trained in discipline, and to be of good speech.

To support mother and father, to cherish wife and children, and to be engaged in peaceful occupation.

To be generous in giving, to be righteous in conduct, to help one's relatives, and to be blameless in action.

To loathe more evil and abstain from it, to refrain from intoxicants, and to be steadfast in virtue.

To be respectful, humble, contented and grateful; and to listen to the Dhamma on due occasions.

To be patient and obedient, to associate with monks and to have religious discussions on due occasions.

Self-restraint, a holy and chaste life, the perception of the Noble Truths and the realisation of Nibbana.

A mind unruffled by the vagaries of fortune, from sorrow freed, from defilements cleansed, from fear liberated.

Those who thus abide, ever remain invincible, in happiness established. These are the greatest blessings."[21]

At the Lumbini relic (Lumbini), where Buddha came to earth. King Ashoka built a 15-meter-high stone pillar, which is still present at this relic with carved his words as

21. The Discourse on Blessings. Mahamangala Sutta.
This Sutta appears in the Sutta-Nipata (v.258ff) and in the Khuddakapatha. See Maha-Mangala Jataka (No. 453). For a detailed explanation see Life's Highest Blessing by Dr. R.L. Soni, WHEEL No. 254/256. https://www.buddhanet.net/e-learning/ethics_m/

following: "After Twenty years after his coronation, King Priyadarsi, (King Asoka's royal title) Beloved of the Gods, visited this place himself and worshiped here saying, here Buddha Sakyamuni was born)."[22]

Additional information is contributed by the Edicts of Ashoka, whose authorship was finally attributed to the Ashoka of Buddhist legend after the discovery of dynastic lists that gave the name used in the edicts (Priyadarshi, "He who regards everyone with affection") as a title or additional name of Ashoka Maurya. Architectural remains of his period have been found at "Kumhrar, PaT.N.a, which include an eighty-pillar hypostyle hall."[23]

At the Deer Park (Sanarth), where the Buddha first rolled the Dharma wheel, King Ashoka also came to worship and erect a very large stone pillar (7 inches in diameter, 15.25 meters high) to marks the place where the Buddha established the Three Jewels, beginning the work of spreading the Dharma.

At Vaishali, an important city in the early days of Buddhism, where the Buddha allowed women to become monks, was the home of the layman Vimalakirti, where Venerable Ananda entered nirvana, Basarh is now about 20 miles northwest of PaT.N.a, between the Ganges River and the Snow Mountains. Right next to the Stupa commemorating the Venerable Ananda, there is a stone pillar erected by King Ashoka to commemorate the Buddha's merit of propagating the Dharma at this place.

Meanwhile, in Sanchi, a city in central India, about 549 miles from Bombay, a place rarely mentioned in Buddhist literature, but surprisingly, King Ashoka himself built a monastery and a Great Stupa at this place with splendid

22. *Lumbini Development Trust, Genesis Publishing, Kathmandu, Nepal/1988*

23. Ayyar, Sulochana. Costume and Ornaments as Depicted in the Early Sculptures of Gwarlior Museum. 186.

and beautiful architecture...

3.10. The Ashoka Lion Capital

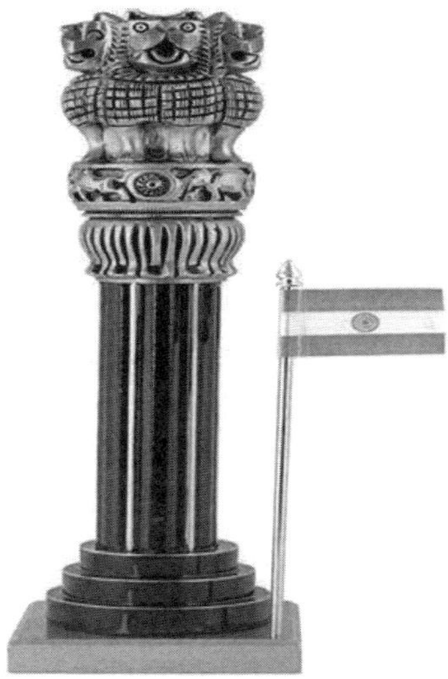

National Emblem and Flag of India

The pillars of Ashoka are "a series of columns dispersed throughout the northern Indian subcontinent and erected by Ashoka during his reign in the third century BCE."[24] Originally, there must have been many pillars of Ashoka although only ten with inscriptions still survive. Averaging between forty and fifty feet in height, and weighing up to fifty tons each, all the pillars were quarried at Chunar, just south of Varanasi and dragged, sometimes hundreds of miles, to where they were erected.

The first Pillar of Ashoka was found in the sixteenth century by Thomas Cory in the ruins. The wheel represents

24. Dharmapal, Maha Thera. Ashoka–2300. Kolkata, India: The Bengal Buddhist Association, 1997. 70, 72.

the sun time and Buddhist law, while the swastika stands for the cosmic dance around a fixed center and guards against evil. The Lion Capital of Ashoka is a sculpture of four lions standing back- to-back. It was originally placed atop the Ashoka pillar at Sarnath, now in the state of Uttar Pradesh, India. The pillar, sometimes called the Ashoka Column, is still in its original location, but the Lion Capital is now in the Sarnath Museum.

This Lion Capital of Ashoka from Sarnath has been adopted as the National Emblem of India and the wheel "Ashoka Chakra" from its base was placed onto the center of the National Flag of India. The capital contains four lions (Indian/Asiatic Lions), standing back-to-back, mounted on an abacus, with a frieze carrying sculptures in high relief of an elephant, a galloping horse, a bull, and a lion, separated by intervening spoked chariot wheels over a bell-shaped lotus. Carved out of a single block of polished sandstone, the capital was believed to be crowned by a "Wheel of Dharma" ("Dharmachakra," popularly known in India as the "Ashoka Chakra").

The Ashoka Lion Capital or the Sarnath Lion Capital is also known as the national symbol of India. The Sarnath pillar bears one of the Edicts of Ashoka, an inscription against division within the Buddhist community, which reads, "No one shall cause division in the order of monks." The Sarnath pillar is a column surmounted by a capital, which consists of a canopy representing an inverted bell-shaped lotus flower, a short cylindrical abacus with four twenty- four-spoked Dharma wheels with four animals (an elephant, a bull, a horse, a lion). The four animals in the Sarnath Capital are believed to symbolize different steps of Lord Buddha's life.The Ashoka Lion capital is displayed at the Archaeological Museum in Sarnath. It is India's national emblem; the national symbol is used in almost all the government documents since ancient times.

The Elephant represents the Buddha's idea in reference to the dream of Queen Maya of a white elephant entering her womb.

- The Bull represents desire during the life of the Buddha as a prince.
- The Horse represents Buddha's departure from palatial life.
- The Lion represents the accomplishment of the Buddha. Besides the religious interpretations, there are some non-religious interpretations of the symbolism of the Ashoka Capital Pillar at Sarnath.

According to them, "the four lions symbolize Ashoka's rule over the four directions; the wheels as symbols of his enlightened rule (Chakravartin) and the four animals are symbols of four adjoining territories of India."[25]

Following is the Dhamma law of piety instilled by Ashoka during his religious administration meant for a nonviolent and peaceful society:

1. Samyam or mastery of senses

25. Chauhan, Giand Chand, Origin and Growth of Feudalism in Early India: From the Mauryas to AD 650. Delhi: Munshiram Manoharlal Publishers, 2004. 186, 192. Mahajan, V.D. Kalinga Rock Edicts–Ancient India. New Delhi: S. Chand and Co. 2008. Ltd. Publishers. 300, 304.

2. Bhavasuddhi or purity of thought
3. Kritajnata or gratitude
4. Dridh-bhakti or steadfasT.N.ess of devotion
5. Daya or kindness
6. Dana or charity
7. Saucha or purity
8. Satya or truthfulness
9. Sushrust or service
10. Sampritipatti or support
11. Apichiti or support (Kalinga Rock Edict xii and xiii).[26]

Ashoka Pillars: a series of columns that are dispersed throughout the Indian subcontinent and carry inscriptions addressed to monks and nuns. Of all the pillars erected by him, there are only twenty of them that still survive. Out of these twenty, only seven well- preserved animal sculptures are present.[27]

---

26. Kiskalar, D.B. "Literary Value of Inscriptions of Ashoka," Journal of Indian History. New Delhi. 226.

27. https://fairgaze.com/fgnews/the-pillars-of-ashoka_92319.html

3.11. King Ashoka was instrumental in organizing the third Buddhist Council

About 218 years after the Buddha entered Nirvana, that is, in 254 B.C., Indian Buddhism developed because of the enthusiastic support of King Ashoka and he also sponsored the organization of the 3rd Buddhsit Council.

Bhikṣuṇī TN Gioi Huong kneels in front of the Sravastī Sacred Site, India, with the King Asoka Litchi stone still intact, September 2003

The Great Emperor Ashoka invited Moggaliputta Tissa, who had attained the three enlightenments and attained Arhatship, to be the chairman and summoned 999

Bhikkhus who had mastered the Tripitaka to participate together. Attended the Great Assembly of Sutras at Pāṭaliputra,[28] so it was called the gathering of 1,000 Arhats.

At the end of this collection, Venerable Maudgalyayana gave the "KathàvatT.N.u", compiled by himself, to explain and clearly distinguish the logic between pagans and Buddhism. This document was later published. included in the Abhidharma Pitaka. The third period of the gathering lasted for nines months, as a result, the Buddha Dharma returned to purity and ordered.

3.12. King Ashoka is credited with spreading Buddhism to Ceylon (Sri Lanka)

Following the 3rd Sutra Council (254 B.C.), King Ashoka sent many delegations to propagate the Dharma abroad such as Ceylon, Burma, Malaysia and Sumatra.

King Ashoka sent his two children, Crown Prince Mahinda and Princess Singhamiha, to become monks and nuns, join the Sangha to study and then were sent to Ceylon to propagate the Dharma around the middle of the century. 3rd BC. The Sanskrit Ashokavadana (Story of Ashoka), written in the second century, and the two Pāli chronicles of Sri Lanka (the Dipavamsa and Mahavamsa), provide most of the currently known information.

3.12.1. Mahā Mahinda Thero (son of King Ashoka) Founded Buddhism for the first time in Ceylon

The third Buddhist council (around 250 BC) in the city of Pataliputta, India, was an important period in the history

28. Pāṭaliputra; P: pāṭaliputta. An ancient city of India, today PaT.N.a. Under King Ashoka, Hoa Thi Thanh was the capital of Magadha (s, p: magadha) and where the third Council conference was held. https://phatgiao.org.vn/tu-dien-phat-hoc-online/hoa-thi-thanh-k949. html

of Buddhism because it was the time when Theravāda Buddhism was transmitted into Sri Lanka. And it was thanks to the merits of King Ashoka that he sent his son, the Holy Monk Mahā Mahinda Thero, and his daughter, the Bhikkhuni Saṅghamittā Theri, to Celon (ancient Sri Lanka) to spread Buddhism.

The history of Sri Lanka's Buddhism began with the day Bhikkhu Thera Mahinda (Sinhala: මිහිඳු මහරහතන් වහන්සේ), son of Emperor Ashoka (Aśoka or Dhammaśoka) came from India to propagate the Dharma in Sri Lanka under reign of King Devānampiya Tissa (236 years after emperor Vijaya). He preached the Dharma to the people, so they could comprehend and receive the message of liberation from Shakyamuni Buddha and quickly apply it in their daily lives.

Painting of Buddhist monk Mahinda bringing Buddhism to Sri Lanka. Artist D. G. Somapala[29]

29. https://www.sundaytimes.lk/180624/funday-times/arahant-mahinda-

From then on, the magical Buddha Dharma spread throughout the island. This shows the compassionate, evangelistic and enlightened energy of the holy monk Arahant Thera Mahinda as stated by His Holiness the World-Honored Buddha: "Bhikkhus, please go to the areas you like, do not Let the two go together. Teach and preach the Dharma to as many people as you can," or "When appearing in the world, bring happiness and peace to the many, for the benefit, for the happiness, for the peace of Gods and humans."[30]

According to the chronicles, Emperor Ashoka and King Devānampiya Tissa (Sri Lanka) were two neighbors who were very close friends, even though they had not met each other face to face. King Devānampiya Tissa often sent important ministers or messengers to bring valuable items to India and in return, King Ashoka also often sent diplomatic missions to Sri Lanka, such as sending his son as Bhikkhu Thera Mahinda came to Sri Lanka to introduce Buddhism with a message full of dharma as follows:

"I have taken refuge with the Buddha (the World-Honored One), with the Dharma Jewel (His teachings), and with the Sangha (the monks in the Congregation). I myself have declared that I am a lay believer in the religion of Shakyamuni Buddha. Now, Your Majesty, oh! You are the most precious person among the people, you have used the Buddha Dharma to transform your mind, take refuge in the Three Jewels (the three most precious persons) among the treasures."

I have taken refuge in the Buddha, his Doctrine and his Order, I have declared myself a lay-disciple in the religion of the Saakya son; seek then, O best of men, refuge in these best of gems, converting your mind with believing

brings-buddhism-to-sri-lanka-299140.html

30. Tăng Chi Bộ I, chương 1, phẩm Một người, phần Như Lai [lược], VNCPHVN ấn hành, 1996, tr 46.

heart.[31]

Aha.m Buddhañ ca Dhammañ ca Sanghañ ca sara. na.mgato upaasakatta.m vedesi.m Saakyaputtassa saasane tvamp'imaani ratanaani uttamaani naruttama citta.m pasaadayitvaana saddhaaya sara.na.m bhaja.

*Sixty-eight practice caves guided by Saint Monk Mahinda.
Photo taken on July 11, 2023*

31. Buddhism in Sri Lanka: A Short History, by H.R. Perera, 2007. https://www.accesstoinsight.org/lib/authors/perera/wheel100.html#sect-47

On the full moon day of the Jetta month, Buddhist calendar year 236 (ie 308 BC, the eighteenth year of King Ashoka's reign), the holy monk Mahā Mahinda along with the Indian missionary team reached the top of Mount Missaka, a high mountain, stands out among the surrounding fertile fields of the present town of Mihintale (8 miles east of the capital Anurādhapura). King Devānampiya Tissa respectfully welcomed the missionary group of the Holy Monk Mahā Mahinda in the capital Anurādhapura. The Cūla Hatthi-padopama Sutta (Majjhima Nikāya, Central Nikāya, 27) is a sermon that Venerable Mahā Mahinda preached to the king about the meaning of taking refuge in the Three Jewels (Buddha, Dharma and Sangha), monastic life, and Vipassana wisdom. After that, the king, along with many officials and people, received the three refuges and five precepts as Buddhist disciples.[32]

The king had a sincere religious heart and arranged for good believers from near and far to come and listen to the teachings of the World-Honored One. The sermon of the Holy Monk Mahā Mahinda has a strong emotional power so that everyone can grasp the Buddha's teachings of compassion and wisdom. Not long after, the Master's message quickly echoed throughout all areas of the island. Buddhism was officially recognized and Bhikkhu Sangha was also established. This is a historical milestone showing that the Theravada Buddhist sect was transmitted out of India and spread to Sri Lanka under the reign of King Devànampiyatissa. Sri Lanka became a center of Buddhism in the world since ancient times.

32. Phật giáo tại Sri Lanka, Piyadassi Manhāthera, Phạm Kim Khánh dịch. https://www.vomonthientu.org/a356/14-phat-giao-tai-sri-lanka-

Photo left to right: Rev. T.N. Vien Nhuan, Dr. Ven. Siri Sumedha, Ven. Dr. T.N. Gioi Huong, Rev. T.N. Vien Bao and Rev. T.N. Vien Lanh, taking photos of the way to the top of Mihintale Great Stupa on July 11, 2023

3.12.2. Bhikkhuni Saṅghamittā Theri (daughter of King Ashoka) founded the Nuns' Order in Ceylon

Queen Anulā, the concubine of a viceroy named Mahānāga, along with 500 maids came to listen to the Dharma, and earnestly asked the holy Venerable Mahinda to become a novice to follow in the footsteps of the Buddha. However, at that time in Ceylon (name of ancient Sri Lanka) there was no Bhikkhuni Order and according to precepts, Venerable Mahinda did not have the right to preside over the ordination ceremony for women, only a Buddha or the Bhikkhuni Order had the right. Therefore, Venerable Mahinda suggested that King Devānampiya Tissa who could request King Ashoka to allow his daughter, Bhikkhuni Saṅghamittā, sister of Venerable Mahinda, who was then a bhikshuni in India, to come to Sri Lanka. held the ordination ceremony for women and established the Bhikkhunī Sangha.

King Devānampiya Tissa happily requested and King Ashoka approved that the princess, Bhikkhuni Saṅghamittā Theri, went to Sri Lanka to preach as nuns. The Holy Patriarch brought with him a Bodhi tree branch extracted from the Bodhi tree by the Nirañjanā River[33] where the World-Honored One meditated for 49 days and attained enlightenment.

King Devānampiya Tissa held an extremely solemn ceremony to receive the sacred Bodhi tree and plant it at Megha Garden, capital Anurādhapura. Currently, the tree is still lush and fresh even after more than 2,600 years and millions of visitors from around the world come here regularly to make pilgrimages and worship. The ancient

33. The Lilājan River (also known by its Sanskrit name: Nirañjanā) is a river that flows through the Chatra and Gaya districts in the Indian states of Jharkhand and Bihar. It is also referred to as the Nilanjan, Niranjana or Falgu Rive. https://en.wikipedia.org/wiki/Lilajan_River

Bodhi tree is recorded as the oldest tree in the world,[34] 2272 years old (2023+249 = 2270 years). From this root, many saplings have been extracted and planted in many monasteries on the island of Sri Lanka and many temples around the world.

Particularly, Elder Bhikkhuni Saṅghamittā Theri is considered the Holy Patriarch of the Nun Sangha in Sri Lankan Buddhism because thanks to her ordaining the Bhikkhuni Order, from which the Bhikkhuni Order was established, exists and develops to this day. So almost all Sri Lankan nun temples worship the statue of the saint Saṅghamittā Theri.

Ven. Dr. T.N. Gioi Huong took a photo with the Nuns in front of the statue the Holy Patriarch Saṅghamittā Their at Susilavasa Temple on July 19, 2023

Therefore, Emperor Ashoka had great merit for sending his son, the crown prince, Bhikkhu Mahinda (Mahendra), to Ceylon to establish Buddhism in the island of Ceylon and later, sent his daughter, Princess Sanghamitra, went to

34. Sri Maha Bodhi – The Sacred Bo Tree http://amazinglanka.com/wp/sri-maha-bodhi-the-sacred-bo-tree/

Sri Lanka to perform the ordination ceremony for nuns, establish the Nun Sangha and spread the path of truth to liberation. Since then, Buddhism, especially Theravada, has developed and become the state religion on the island of Sri Lanka.

3.13. Death and Legacy

Ashoka's Major Rock Edict at Junagadh contains inscriptions by Ashoka (fourteen of the Edicts of Ashoka), Rudradaman I, and Skandagupta. Ashoka ruled for an estimated thirty-six years. Legend states that during his cremation, his body burned for seven days and nights. After his death, the Mauryan Dynasty lasted just fifty more years until his empire stretched over almost all of the Indian subcontinent.

Ashoka had many wives and children, but many of their names are lost to time. His chief consort (agramahisi) for the majority of his reign was his wife, Asandhimitra, who apparently bore him no children. In his old age, he seems to have come under the spell of his youngest wife, Tishyaraksha. It is said that she had Ashoka's son Kunala, the regent in Takshashila and the heir presumptive to the throne, blinded by a wily stratagem. The official executioners spared Kunala and he became a wandering singer accompanied by his favorite wife, Kanchanmala. In Pataliputra, Ashoka heard Kunala's song, and realized that Kunala's misfortune may have been a punishment for some past sin of the emperor himself. He condemned Tishyaraksha to death, restoring Kunala to the court. In the Ashokavadana, Kunala is portrayed as forgiving Tishyaraksha, having obtained enlightenment through Buddhist practice. While he urges "Ashoka to forgive her as well, Ashoka does not respond with the same forgiveness. Kunala was succeeded by his son, Samprati, who ruled for fifty years until his death."[35]

Asoka, is the Indian Hindi-language epic historical drama film from 2001, in which the famous star, Shah Rukh Khan, played the role of Ashoka with actress Kareena Kapoor playing his wife. The film describes that Emperor Asoka was one of the great moral reformers in the history of civilization and a precocious pioneer of humanitarian values in his rule.

More than two thousand six hundred years have passed, King Ashoka's contributions still have a strong influence on the lives of Indian people in particular and Buddhism in general.

Most notably, the national emblem and flag of India, the stone pillars and the Dharma wheel in the Deer Park, Sarnath, Varanasi, India of King Ashoka, are still familiar symbols to the people. King Ashoka is a disciple of Buddha, a devout follower of Buddhism, a monarch who upholds the Dharma, uses the precepts (Ten Virtues) and the Six Harmonies to guide the masses towards the

35. Bandarkar, B.R. Ashoka. Kolkata. Calcutta University, 1999. 87, 89.

good path, enlightenment and liberation. From then on, the wheel of Dharma will roll forever to bring the light of Buddha's compassion and wisdom to people everywhere in the world.

IV. HISTORY OF Vietnam AND BUDDHISM

4.1. First Human Evidence

Archaeological excavations have revealed the existence of humans in what is now Vietnam as early as the Paleolithic Age. "Homo erectus fossils dating to around 500,000 BC have been found in caves in Lạng Sơn and Nghệ An Provinces in northern Vietnam."[36]

4.2. Paleolithic to Neolithic

By about 1000 BC, the development of wet-rice cultivation and bronze casting in the Ma River and Red River floodplains led to the flourishing of the Đông Sơn culture, notable for its elaborate bronze drums. At this time, "the early Vietnamese kingdoms of Văn Lang and Âu Lạc appeared, and the culture's influence spread to other parts of Southeast Asia, including Maritime Southeast Asia throughout the first millennium BC."16

People appeared in Vietnam about 10,000–30,000 years ago with vestiges of the Núi Đọ, Thần Sa, Sơn Vi. New Age was typical with Hòa Bình, Bắc Sơn cultures about 6,000–10,000 years ago and the Metal Age was about 4,000 years ago.

36. https://www.indochinavalue.com/Vietnam-travel-guide/Vietnamese-history/prehistoric-vieT.Nam
https://giaoduc.net.vn/ten-goi-viet-nam-co-tu-khi-nao-post189425.gd

4.3. The National Name of Vietnam

Kinh Dương Vương is the ancestor of the Vietnamese nation. The Văn Lang country lasted for nearly 2,000 years, through eighteen Hùng kings and the capital was located in Phong Châu.

The Thục Dynasty (257–208 BC) took the country name Âu Lạc, stationed the capital in Cổ Loa. The Triệu Dynasty (207–111 BC) occupied Âu Lạc, and changed the country's name to Nam Việt. The Hán Dynasty (111 BC–39) occupied Nam Việt and changed it to Giao Chỉ. "Vietnam," the national name of Vietnam officially appeared in the Nguyễn Dynasty and was proclaimed in 1804. When the August Revolution of 1945 succeeded on September 2, 1945, when "President Hồ Chí Minh read the Declaration of Independence giving birth to the Democratic Republic of Vietnam (Việt Nam Dân chủ Cộng hòa), the national name of Vietnam was officially recognized."

Vietnam Geography Map

Vietnam was part of Imperial China for over a millennium, from 111 BC to AD 939. An independent Vietnamese state was formed in 939, following a Vietnamese victory in the Battle of Bạch Đằng River.

Successive Vietnamese royal dynasties flourished as the nation expanded geographically and politically into Southeast Asia, until the Indochina Peninsula was colonized by the French in the mid-nineteenth century.Following a Japanese occupation in the 1940s, the Vietnamese fought French rule in the First Indochina War, eventually expelling the French in 1954. Thereafter, Vietnam was divided politically into two rival states, North and South Vietnam. Conflict between the two sides intensified in what is known as the Vietnam War. The war ended with a North Vietnamese victory in 1975.

Vietnam was then unified but remained impoverished and politically isolated. In 1986, Vietnam carried out economic renovation and foreign policy reform with the motto of wanting to be friends with all countries. As a result, Vietnam's economy, politics, and society has become more and more stable and developed. Currently, Vietnam is enjoying peace after a long history of struggle to build and defend the country.

4.4. Buddhism in Viet Nam

Buddhism in Vietnam (in Vietnamese called đạo Phật or Phật giáo) as practiced by the ethnic Vietnamese is mainly of the Mahāyāna tradition. Buddhism may have first come to Vietnam as early as the third or second century BCE from South Asia or from China in the first or second century CE. Vietnamese Buddhism has had a symbiotic relationship with certain elements of Taoism, Chinese spirituality, and the Vietnamese folk religion.

There are conflicting theories regarding whether Buddhism first reached Vietnam during the third or second century BCE via delegations from India, or during the first or second century from China. In either case, by the end of the second century CE, Vietnam had developed into a major regional Mahāyāna Buddhist center centering on

Luy Lâu in modern Bắc Ninh Province, northeast of the present-day capital city of Hanoi. Luy Lâu was the capital of the Hán region of Jiaozhi (Giao Chỉ) and was a popular place visited by many Indian Buddhist missionary monks en route to China. The monks followed "the maritime trade route from the Indian sub-continent to China used by Indian traders. A number of Mahāyāna sutras and the āgamas were translated into Classical Chinese there, including the Sutra of Forty-Two Chapters and the Anapanasati Sutra."[37]

Indian Prime Minister N. D. Modi visited Quán Sứ Temple in Hà Nội in 2016

Over the next eighteen centuries, Vietnam and China shared many common features of cultural, philosophical, and religious heritage. This was due to geographical proximity and Vietnam being annexed twice by China. Vietnamese Buddhism is thus related to Chinese Buddhism

37. Nguyễn Lang (aka Zen Master Thích Nhất Hạnh), Việt Nam Phật giáo Sử luận, tập 1,2,3. 1973. https://langmai.org/tang-kinh-cac/vien-sach/giang-kinh/viet-nam-phat-giao-su-luan/chuong-12-tran-nhan-tong-va-thien-phai-truc-lam/

in general, and to some extent reflects the formation of Chinese Buddhism after the Song Dynasty.

Theravāda Buddhism, on the other hand, would become incorporated through the southern annexation of Khmer people and territories. During the Đinh Dynasty (968–980), Buddhism was recognized by the state as an official faith (971), reflecting the high esteem of Buddhist faith held by the Vietnamese monarchs. The Early Lê dynasty (980–1009) also afforded the same recognition to the Buddhist church. The growth of Buddhism during this time is attributed to the recruitment of erudite monks to the court as the newly independent state needed an ideological basis on which to build a country. Subsequently, this role was ceded to Confucianism. Vietnamese Buddhism reached its zenith during the Lý dynasty (1009–1225) beginning with the founder Lý Thái Tổ, who was raised in a pagoda. All of the kings during the Lý dynasty professed and sanctioned Buddhism as the state religion. This endured with "the Trần Dynasty (1225–1400) but Buddhism had to share the stage with the emerging growth of Confucianism."[38]

By the fifteenth century, Buddhism fell out of favor with the court during the later Lê dynasty, although still popular with the masses. Officials like Lê Quát attacked it as heretical and wasteful. It was not until the nineteenth century that Buddhism regained some stature under the Nguyễn dynasty who accorded royal support.

The Thiền school, founded by Trần Nhân Tông King (1258– 1308), was named the Trúc Lâm (meaning "Bamboo Grove" Zen sect). This revealed a deep influence of Confucian and Taoist philosophy. Nevertheless, Trúc Lâm's prestige waned over the following centuries as

38. Lê Văn Hưu, Phan Phu Tiên, Ngô Sĩ Liên. Đại Việt Sử Ký Toàn Thư (National Bureau for Historical Records). 1993, P. 182. Viện Khoa Học Xã Hội Việt Nam dịch (1985–1992). https://www.tuvienquangduc.com.au/lichsu/lichsuVietnam/Daivietsukytoanthu. pdf

Confucianism became dominant in the royal court. In the seventeenth century, a group of Chinese monks, led by Nguyên Thiều, introduced the Ling school (Lâm Tế). A more domesticated offshoot of Lâm Tế, the Liễu Quán school was founded in the eighteenth century and has since been a branch of Vietnamese Zen. Since the twentieth and twenty-first century Zen Master Thích Thanh Từ has been restored to the Trúc Lâm Zen Sect by founding hundreds of Trúc Lâm Zen monasteries in Vietnam and abroad, especially the predominant Yên Tử Mount (Quảng Ninh) where the Trần Nhân Tông Zen founder resided and spread the Vietnamese Zen.

Buddhism has been present in Vietnam for over 2,600 years, associated with the ups and downs of the nation's destiny, from the time of Hùng Vương, Chư Đồng Tử – Tiên Dung, Hai Bà Trưng, Ngô Quyền, Lý Dynasty (1010–1225), Trần reign (1225–1400), Lê Dynasty (1418–1527), Trịnh-Nguyễn (1533–1788), Nguyễn (1802–1883), and Pháp đô hộ (1883–1945) to currently. Buddhism with its moral doctrine of doing good, avoiding evil, and keeping the mind pure still exist in the nation as poet Huyền Không said:

The roof of the pagoda protects the soul of the nation

It is the eternal living way of our ancestors.

(Remember the Pagoda – Huyền Không)

Mái Chùa che chở hồn dân tộc

Nếp sống muôn đời của tổ tiên.

(Nhớ Chùa – Huyền Không)

Especially through the dynasties of Đinh, Lê, Lý, Trần, Trịnh, Nguyễn... Buddhism developed to its peak and many monks became the National Masters for the Vietnamese Kings, advising and planning national development programs such as Venerable Khuông Việt, the chief of Sangha, Ngô Chân Lưu, Zen Master Vạn Hạnh, the skilled Zen poet Tuệ Trung Thượng Sỹ, King Trần Thái Tông, the Trúc Lâm Zen Founder – King Trần Nhân Tông, and so on.

V. TRẦN NHÂN TÔNG EMPEROR (1258–1308)

5.1. Since Childhood, He Had the Golden Buddha Signs

Trần Nhân Tông, the third emperor of the Trần Dynasty of Vietnam, was born on December 7, 1258 (Novermber 11 of the Lunar Calender 1258). His birth name was Trần Khâm. He was the first son of the Emperor Trần Thánh Tông.[39]

The Golden Buddha Trần Nhân Tông,
the first Trúc Lâm Zen Founder

39. Việt Nam Phật Giáo Sử Luận (History of Vietnam Buddhism), tập 1,2,3. Nguyễn Lang (aka Zen Master Thích Nhất Hạnh), Lá Bối. 1973. https://langmai.org/tang-kinh-cac/vien-sach/giang-kinh/viet-nam-phat-giao-su- luan/chuong-12-tran-nhan-tong-va-thien-phai-truc-lam/

It was said that the newborn Trần Khâm had the elite sign of the saints, such as the pure gold physique and the bright perfect manner. Both signs are considered signs of a heavenly extraordinary appearance. His grandfather Thái Tông and father Thánh Tông named him "Kim Tiên Đồng Tử (Pupil of the Heaven)."[40] Due to these good generals, he was also honored as "the Golden Buddha" (Phật Hoàng), Phật Hoàng Trần Nhân Tông ever since he was a child.

5.2. Wanting to Give Up His Position as King and Become a Monastic

Prince Trần Khâm was entitled as crown prince of the Trần Dynasty in December 1274 (sixteen years old). The Emperor himself also composed poems and a literary work called Di Hậu Lục (Two Books). He taught the crown prince how to behave in order to prepare for the future king and the faiths, so the prince became a master of the Three Religions (Buddhism, Taoism, and Confucianism). However, Trần Khâm was fond of a Buddhist life and had followed Zen since his childhood. At the age of sixteen, he was anointed crown prince. He tried to "yield the royal role to his younger brother but his father King Trần Thánh Tông refused his attempt."[41]

His father king Trần Thánh Tông forced his crown prince son to marry the eldest daughter of Nguyên Từ Quốc Mẫu. His wife later had the title of Khâm Tộ Thái Hậu.

In the royal palace with his wife, he lived in comfort

40. Book Tam Tổ Thực Lục called "The Golden Buddha" (Phật Hoàng). Ibid.
https://langmai.org/tang-kinh-cac/vien-sach/giang-kinh/viet-nam- phat-giao-su- luan/chuong-12-tran-nhan-tong-va-thien-phai-truc-lam/

41. Lê Văn Hưu, Phan Phu Tiên, Ngô Sĩ Liên. 1993. 18

and happiness but always thought of leading an ascetic life by becoming a monk. One must remember that this was the same grand thinking and ambition that prince Siddharta had to lead a non-attached, non-worldly life. Further, like Prince Siddharta he left his royal palace in search of truth at midnight of a full moon day, leaving his wife Yasodhara and child Rahula. This is known as the great renunciation. The prince later became Sakyamuni Buddha, the Enlightened One. Trần Nhân Tông also, "One night at the time of the Rat, climbed out of the citadel, which had most comforts of the world, and fled towards Yên Tử mountain. There he approached Tháp Temple at the Đông Cửu Mountain. When it was morning, he immediately went to hide in the tower and lay down for a rest."[42]

The head monk of the temple made a meal for the guest as the stranger had an extraordinary appearance. The head monk recognized him and sent the message to the king. The army unit deployed by the king traced him and made him return to the palace. So due to his father and the sense of heavy duty for country, the prince returned to the worldly life to keep the royal lineage.

5.3. Even as King, He Kept a Vegetarian Diet and Practiced Zen

At the age of twenty-one (in 1279), he was crowned emperor, alias Trần Nhân Tông. Although in a noble position, he still kept himself pure, vegtarian, eating one time a day at noon and he often went to Từ Phước pagoda to practice.

In the year of leaving home, the king invited Văn Túc Vương Đạo Tái (son of Trần Quang Khải) to join him for lunch. Being very fond of Văn Túc Vương Đạo Tái, the

42. Lê Văn Hưu, Phan Phu Tiên, Ngô Sĩ Liên. 1993. 195.

king invited Dao Tai to vist at Dưỡng Đức building in Thánh Từ Palace and sent a person to serve the dishes to invite Đạo Tái. The king was already a vegetarian, so he just sat and watched Đạo Tái eating the non-vegetarian meal. The king wrote the following poem:

The meat is crimson token
The dish smells
and looks taste
I am a mountain monk who keeps pure
precepts Sitting together but not eating together.

(Món quy cước đỏ
thắm Món mã yên
vàng thơm Sơn tăng
giữ tịnh giới
Cùng ngồi không cùng ăn)[43]

Even if the king hadn't ordained, he still considered himself a "mountain monk." He cherished his will to be a monastic and prepared for his ordination.

There was another significant event in his life. One day on lunch break, he dreamed that in his navel grew a golden lotus the size of a wheel, on which there was a golden Buddha. Someone stood beside him and said, "Do you know this Buddha? That's the Virtue Transformation!". When he woke up, he brought it up to his father, King Thánh Tông, who cried and persuaded his son to live the royal life, to postpone his monastic life as below:

43. Việt Nam Phật Giáo Sử Luận (History of Vietnam Buddhism), tập 1,2,3. Nguyễn Lang (aka Zen Master Thích Nhất Hạnh), Lá Bối. 1973. https://langmai.org/tang-kinh-cac/vien-sach/giang-kinh/viet-nam-phat-giao-su- luan/chuong-12-tran-nhan-tong-va-thien-phai-truc-lam/

The Book of Tam Tổ Thực Lục[44] says: "Although he sat on nine layers of glorious pedestals, his life was very pure. One day napping at Từ Phước pagoda in the inner city, Trần Nhân Tông King dreamed that on his navel bloomed a lotus as large as a wheel, on which was a golden Buddha. Beside him, someone pointed to the king and asked: Do you know this Buddha? That's the Virtue Transformation! The king woke up, brought the dream back to Thánh Tông, and everyone was surprised. Ever since, he was often vegetarian to avoid meat and fish, and his face was so emaciated. Thánh Tông found his son, who still favored the monastic life, cried and said: 'I am old, I rely on you alone, if you are like that, how can I continue the prosperity of my ancestors?' Trần Nhân Tông King also cried and he accepted to keep the throne while learning Buddhism."[45]

He was compassionate, insightful, and multitalented, reading all kinds of scriptures through both internal (Buddhist studies) and secular texts, and often inviting Buddhist masters to come and lecture on Zen studies. He also consulted with Tuệ Trung Thượng Sĩ, and thus penetrated the essence of Zen, so he often took his humble position of a disciple to treat Tuệ Trung as his teacher.

5.4. Three Times Victories over Mongolian–Yuan Invaders to Protect Country

The Emperor Trần Nhân Tông and his father, the retired Emperor Trần Thánh Tông, were credited as the supreme commanders who led the Trần Dynasty to the three victories over Mongolian (Mông) and Chinese Yuan

44. Việt Nam Phật Giáo Sử Luận (History of Vietnam Buddhism), tập 1,2,3. Nguyễn Lang (aka Zen Master Thích Nhất Hạnh), Lá Bối. 1973. https://langmai.org/tang-kinh-cac/vien-sach/giang-kinh/viet-nam-phat-giao-su- luan/chuong-12-tran-nhan-tong-va-thien-phai-truc-lam/

45. Ibid.

(Nguyên) invaders and established a long period of peace and prosperity over the country.

Firstly, the Mongols attacked Đại Việt in February 1258. From Đại Lý, about 15,000–25,000 Mongol cavalry and 20,000 Đại Lý troops (a total of about 35,000–45,000 men) entered Đại Việt.

Secondly, twenty-seven years later, the Yuan Emperor Kublai Khan (Hốt Tất Liệt) ordered the invasion of Đại Việt. This war lasted from the end of December of the Monkey Year to the end of April of the year of the Rooster (the end of January to the end of May 1285 of the solar calendar). This time, the Yuan army prepared for the war better, mobilizing a much larger force, up to tens of thousands of troops. In addition to the army coming down from the north, there were also marines from the Chiêm Thành front in the south to support.

Thirdly, immediately after the defeat, returning China in 1287, the Yuan army reorganized and supplemented their forces to take revenge. Learning from previous defeats, the Yuan forces built many food ships by sea to return to fight Đại Việt for the third time. This war lasted about four months, from the end of December 1287 to the end of April 1288.

In the beginning of the war, Thánh Tông and Nhân Tông had to order the skilled army to retreat to avoid the pressure from Yuan's force when Prince Chiêu Minh Trần Quang Khải commanded troops try to stop Sogetu's fleet in the Nghệ An Province. During this time, there were several high-ranking officials and members of royal family of the Trần Dynasty who defected to Yuan's side, including Thánh Tông's own brother, Prince Chiêu Quốc Trần Ích Tắc, and Trần Kiện who was son of Prince Tĩnh Quốc Trần Quốc Khang.

Dealing with the threat from the north, in October 1282, the retired Emperor Trần Thánh Tông and the

Emperor Trần Nhân Tông gathered all members of the royal family and officials in the royal court to discuss the unadvoidable war. In 1283, Hưng Đạo Vương (real name Trần Quốc Tuấn) was appointed as "commander- in-chief (Quốc công Tiết Chế) of Đại Việt Army, and the retired Emperor and the Emperor began to hold military exercises with their generals and troops."[46]

To build the whole nation into a strong national resistance the emperor listened to the ideas from experienced persons. He held a conference of the military generals at Bình Than, and then a conference of the old sages at Diên Hồng. For example, under the smart plan of Nhân Tông. "In the Horse Year, fourth year [1282], in the winter, in October, King Nhân Tông went to Bình Than to stay in Trần Xá village to meet the royal court and hundreds of mandarins, to discuss skillfully crafting plans and dividing up to keep dangerous places wisely."

The first invasion of the Mongols was just stone-throwing. Despite being smashed by the Trần Dynasty, the greatest danger was still there. Thirty years later, the giant army of invaders on both land and water of the Yuan Mongolian Empire, at its peak after knocking down the Southern Song Dynasty, entered our country with an imperceptible momentum, and we could not resist. However, a benevolent Zen master Nhân Tông' Kind who did not want to be a king, along with his small army, calmly defeated the Chinese and Mongolian army of "the wrath of God."[47]

On May 10 of the lunar calendar 1285, Trần Quang Khải fought the decisive battle in Chương Dương where Sogetu's navy was almost destroyed and therefore the balance in the battlefield tilted definitely in favor of the

46. Lê Văn Hưu, Phan Phu Tiên, Ngô Sĩ Liên. 1993. 195.

47. https://vi.wikipedia.org/wiki/Chi%E1%BA%BFn_tranh_Nguyen-Mong

Trần Dynasty. Ten days after Sogetu was killed and Trần's Emperor Nhân Tông and retired Emperor Thánh Tông returned to the capital of Thăng Long on June 6 of lunar calendar, 1285.

In March 1287, the Yuan dynasty launched their third invasion of Đại Việt. Unlike the second attack, this time Commander in Chief Hưng Đạo Vương (Trần Quốc Tuấn) affirmed with the emperor that Đại Việt's army could easily break Yuan's military campaign. Indeed, this invasion was ended one year later by a disastrous defeat of the Yuan Navy at the Battle of Bạch Đằng on March 8 of lunar calendar, 1288. Besides Trần Quốc Tuấn, other notable generals of the Trần dynasty during this time were Nhân Huệ Vương (Trần Khánh Dư) who destroyed the logistics convoy of the Yuan Navy in the Battle of Vân Đồn or general Phạm Ngũ Lão, who took charge of ambushing Prince Toghan's retreating troops.

The critical situation of the Trần dynasty began to change after their victory in the Battle of Hàm Tử in April 1285, where the troops commanded by Trần Nhật Duật, Prince Chiêu Thành, Trần Quốc Toản, and Nguyễn Khoái were finally able to defeat the fleet of Sogetu. In rewarding the Trần Dynasty generals and mandarins after the victory, "Thánh Tông and Nhân Tông also reminded them to be cautious of the northern border."[48]

The Monglian Yuan-Đại Việt War or the Resistance War against the Mongol invaders was a war to protect the Fatherland of Đại Việt troops and people in the early Trần Dynasty under the Trần Thánh Tông and Trần Nhân Tông King s. Although the time of the resistance war was from 1258 to 1288, the official war time only included about nine months in total, divided into three phases of the first, second, and third wars which were the times of active diplomacy. As a result, these three resistance wars

48. Chapuis. 1995. 84–85. 32. Ngô Sĩ Liên. 1993.19

are considered as one of the most heroic historical pages of the Vietnamese nation, and also a typical feat of the Trần Dynasty.

Ever since, it can be said Nhân Tông was a true Buddhist cultivator with widespread compassion, and also a wise hero in Vietnam history. Not only did he manage the country strongly, defeating two invasions of the most terrible Mongolian Army in the world, but he also expanded the territory of two continents for Vietnam as well as deepening his spiritual practice.

5.5. Trần Nhân Tông King Became a Monk and Founder of Trúc Lâm Zen School

In 1293, Trần Nhân Tông yielded the kingship to his son, Trần Anh Tông, and mentored the new king for six years. In 1299, he entered the monkhood at Ngọa Vân Am, in the bamboo forest on Yên Tử Mountain where he practiced strictly as a twelve-ascetic precept-holder,[49]

49. 12 ascetic precepts: (1) Garments of cast-off rags. (2) To wear only three garments. (3) Eat only food begged. (4) Eat only breakfast and the main noon meal. (5) No food between breakfast and the noon meal. (6) Eat with limited amount, only eat what you have in the begging bowl without asking for more. (7) Dwelling as a hermit. (8) Dwelling among tombs. (9) Dwelling under a tree. (10) Dwelling under the open sky. (11)

so He was called "A Great Ascetic of Fragrant Clouds (means Hương Vân Đại Đầu Đà)."[50]

View of the birthplace of Trúc Lâm Zen School, Yên Tử Mount, Quảng Ninh

Some time after ordination, Hương Vân Đại Đầu Đà founded the Trúc Lâm (Bamboo Grove) Zen School on Yên Tử Mount. It is the only native school of Buddhism in Vietnam showing influences from Confucian and Taoist philosophy. This is a type of worldly Buddhist Zen as he was still engaged the politics of the royal court and still maintained his spiritual practice (secular and supersecular at the same time). He became the sixth patriarch of the Yên Tử Sect and the first ancestor of the Trúc Lâm Zen Sect. He also had other names such as Trúc Lâm, Great Ascetic (Trúc Lâm Đại Đầu Đà), Trúc Lâm Great Monk (Trúc Lâm Đại Sĩ) and the Golden Buddha Controller

Dwelling anywhere. (12) Sitting and not lying down.

50. Lê Văn Hưu, Phan Phu Tiên, Ngô Sĩ Liên. Đại Việt Sử Ký Toàn Thư (National Bereau for Historical Record). Viện Khoa Học Xã Hội Việt Nam dịch (1985 - 1992). 1993. https://www.tuvienquangduc.com. au/lichsu/lichsuVietnam/Daivietsukytoanthu. pdf

(Giác Hoàng Điều Ngự).[51]

In Yên Tử Mount, he opened a vihara, lectured for monastics, and gained quite a number of disciples.

Trúc Lâm Buddhism played the role as the the Engaged Buddhism, closely related to politics, culture, and society. The Trúc Lâm Buddhists were very suitable for such a movement and that is the main reason why this Zen school was founded. The Yên Tử Buddhist tradition and Trúc Lâm's appearance has brought a lot of social character and entered the world, so it is natural and reasonable to use a new title for the new sect in fourteenth-century Vietnam.

In the sixth-thirteenth centuries, Đại Việt existed mainly based on three Zen lines of Tỳ-Ni-Đa-Luu-Chi (Vinītaruci)[52] Vô Ngôn Thông[53] and Thảo Đường.[54]

Crown Prince Trần Khâm, later King Trần Nhân Tông, was sent by King Trần Thánh Tông to Tuệ Trung Thượng Sĩ to study morality. Before returned his palace, the prince asked, "What is the main goal of meditation?" Tuệ Trung Thượng Sĩ replied, "Reflecting on self-discipline is the main duty, avoiding running outside," that is, turning

51. Ibid.

52. In the 6th century, the Patriarch Vinītaruci went from India to China to study Buddhism with the Patriarch Tăng Xán. After attaining enlightenment, he was taught by the Patriarch Tăng Xán to go to the South to spread Zen Buddhism, so he went to Vietnam to stay at Dâu Pagoda.

53. In the 9th century, there was Zen Master Vô Ngôn Thôn, a disciple of Bá Trượng's ancestor in China, who went to Vietnam to transmit meditation, so there was Vô Ngôn ThônZen sect.

54. There was Master Thảo Đường, when the Ly dynasty conquered Champa, captured a number of officials and brought them back to Vietnam, including him. Only in Thăng Long did he discover that he was a Zen master, since then the kings and mandarins of the Lý Dynasty admired and respected him and he became the Patriarch of the Thảo Đường Zen sect in Vietnam.

back to reflect on oneself, that is the main duty to attain enlightenment, nothing else, nothing from the outside.

After enthronement, Trần Nhân Tông King both took care of the governance of the country and studied the internal scriptures, without ever neglecting either. At the throne for a while, seeing that there was an heir, at the age of forty-one, he gave all power to his son and left home. He went to Yên Tử mountain to practice. After five years of practicing asceticism in the bamboo forest, he was completely enlightened to the Way. Since then, he spread the word and founded the Trúc Lâm Yên Tử Zen Sect.

"The Trúc Lâm Yên Tử sect was born, including the three quintessences of the three sects of Vinītaruci, Vô Ngôn Thông, and Thảo Đường, agglomerating into a pure Vietnamese Zen Sect."[55] Since Trúc Lâm Yên Tử sect was born, the other sects have been absent and no longer developed. This is considered the first unified Buddhist church in Vietnam.

Trúc Lâm Zen Sect acquires "the foundation of South Asian Buddhism and Đông Độ (Indian) meditation, while using Vietnamese cultural values and encouraging Buddhists to contribute to society on the basis of the compassion and wisdom of Buddhism. Master Trúc Lâm himself not only settled in Yên Tử, but also lectured many

55.http://thuongchieu.net/index.php/phapthoai/suong/1960-pht-giao-thin-tong-vit-nam

pagodas such as Phổ Minh (Thiên Trường), Sùng Nghiêm (Chí Linh), Vĩnh Nghiêm (Yên Dũng) và Báo Ân – Siêu Loại (nay thuộc Gia Lâm, Hà Nội)."[56]

5.6. Forming a Buddhist-Based Society

To support Đại Việt and learn the scriptures of the Buddha, in the second lunar month of 1295, Master Trúc Lâm sent the foreign ministers Trần Khắc Dụng and Phạm Thảo to Yuan Chinese Dynasty to request the Great Tripitaka (Sutras, Vinaya, and Abhidharma). This request was approved by Nguyên Thành Tông. The sutras brought back by the mission were kept in Thiên Trường palace, and in addition, the emperor ordered the copy to be printed for circulation in the country.

In 1304, Master Hương Vân Đại Đầu Đà (Trần Nhân Tông) traveled around the country, encouraging his people to quit worshipping sexual gods and to abandon wrong views. He taught the ten good deeds, (1) not to kill, (2) not to steal, (3) to refrain from all sexual activity, (4) not to lie, (5) not to drink intoxicants, (6) not to wear ornaments or perfume, (7) not to listen to singing or watch dancing,

(8) not to sleep on an elevated or broad bed, (9) not to eat at an improper hour, i.e., after noon, and (10) not to own valuables such as gold and silver. He still gave advice on some political issues, and advised Anh Tông King "to give up alcohol and make often offerings and supported the monks."[57]

Ten Precepts is the basic teaching of Buddhism, the basis for social ethics. Trúc Lâm had the intention to build a society on the basis of Buddhist morality. A young king sat on the throne in support of Buddhism, a king who worked as a monk to travel among the masses. This event

56. https://terebess.hu/zen/mesterek/Tran-Nhan-Tong.htm\

57. https://terebess.hu/zen/mesterek/Tran-Nhan-Tong.html

is unique and unprecedented. Whether "consciously or not, Trúc Lâm also contributed to the consolidation of the dynasty and regime by active religious practices in the folk."[58]

In the winter of the same year, 1304, King Trần Anh Tông requested that Master Hương Vân Đại Đầu Đà visit the royal citadel and transmit the Bodhisattva Precepts for laywomen and laymen. Aterwards, he came to reside at Sùng Nghiêm Temple in Linh Sơn Mountain, where he performed the Bodhisattva ordination and taught Zen to the general public.

The monarchs who took the bodhisattva ordination were those who vowed to use the ability and power of their royal position to serve people based on the bodhisattva's conduct. On the day Trúc Lâm Zen Master entered the citadel, the kings and officers followed the king to welcome National Master Trúc Lâm. Seeing that King Trần Anh Tông made a vow to take the bodhisattva precepts, they also took Refuge in the Triple Gem (following the way of Buddha, dharma, and sangha) and keeping Five Precepts (abstaining from killing living beings, stealing, sexual misconduct, lying and intoxication). In terms of formality,

58. Việt Nam Phật giáo Sử luận (History of Vietnam Buddhism), tập 1,2,3. Nguyễn Lang (aka Zen Master Thích Nhất Hạnh), Lá Bối. 1973. https://langmai.org/tang-kinh-cac/vien-sach/giang-kinh/viet-nam-phat-giao-su- luan/chuong-12-tran-nhan-tong-va-thien-phai-truc-lam/

an entire court became Buddhist and a Buddhist-based society with their citizens living a moral life as their kings and ancestors.

5.7. The Second Ancestor of the Trúc Lâm Zen Sect

The first ancestor, Trúc Lâm, was an example of a talented and virtuous sangha leader and emperor. During his time traveling in the human world, Trúc Lâm also intended to find a dharma successor, that is, a person who could continue his career of preaching in the world.

In 1304, when he came to Nam Sách village, Trúc Lâm met a young man, twenty-one years old, who wanted to become a monk, named Đồng Kiên Cương. Seeing his unusual appearance, Trúc Lâm said to himself, "This young man has an insight vision and in the future will surely become a dharma preacher." Happy because of this meeting, Trúc Lâm named him Thiện Lai, gave him the novice ordination, and sent him to study with the Most Venerable Tính Giác. Thiện Lai later became Pháp Loa, the second patriarch of the Trúc Lâm Zen Sect.

Pháp Loa only worked as a novice for over a year. In 1305, Trúc Lâm gave him ordination as a bhikkhu and as a bodhisattva. In 1306, he was appointed a dharma lecturer at Siêu Loại Pagoda. The first ancestor himself taught Pháp Loa from historical Buddhist books such as Truyền Đăng Lục I (Record of Transmission of the Lamp) and Đại Tuệ Ngữ Lục (The Great Insight Dharma Sentences).[59]

5.8. Monastic Disciples and Lineage of the Trúc Lâm Zen Sect

Besides Pháp Loa, the Trúc Lâm's second successor, the Patriach Trúc Lâm, also had other monastic disciples

59 Ibid.

such as Bảo Sát, Bảo Phác, Pháp Không, Pháp Cổ và Huệ Nghiêm. In addition, according to the chart of Huệ Nghiêm in the book, Tuệ Trung Thượng Sĩ Ngữ Lục, among Trúc Lâm's disciples were Pháp Tràng, Hương Tràng, Hương Sơn, and Mật Tạng.

5.9. Lineage of Trúc Lâm Zen School

Zen Buddhism has been up and down following the fate of the country, however, according to the book, Lý-Trần Dynasty's Literature (Thơ Văn Lý Trần),[60] the Trúc Lâm Zen School has a long list of successors' transmission of the Zen lamp genre and upspring in the twentieth and twenty-first century as below:

1. Zen Master Trần Nhân Tông aka Hương Vân đại đầu đà (1258–1308)
2. Zen Master Pháp Loa (1284–1330)
3. Zen Master Huyền Quang (1254–1334)
4. Zen Master An Tâm
5. Zen Master Phù Vân Tĩnh Lự
6. Zen Master Vô Trước
7. Zen Master Quốc Nhất
8. Zen Master Viên Minh
9. Zen Master Đạo Huệ
10. Zen Master Viên Ngộ
11. Zen Master Tổng Trì
12. Zen Master Khuê Sâm
13. Zen Master Sơn Đăng

1. 14. Zen Master Hương Sơn

60. Thơ Văn Lý Trần. Nguyễn Huệ Chi. NXB Khoa Học Xã Hội. Hà Nội 1988. File DPF.

15. Zen Master Trí Dung
16. Zen Master Huệ Quang
17. Zen Master Chân Trụ
18. Zen Master Vô Phiền . . .
19. Zen Master Thanh Từ (twentieth-twenty-first centuries)...

5.10. Works of Trần Nhân Tông King

As the Trúc Lâm Zen master who realized enlightenment and as the king who loved his countries, Trần Nhân Tông King was pained when the foreign invaders came to attack Đại Việt. He wrote many edicts, prose, and poems to express his heart and feeling for the country and Buddhism as below:

- Thiền lâm thiết chủy ngữ lục (Zen Sentences)
- Tăng già toái sự (The Daily Troubles of Monastics)
- Thạch thất mỵ ngữ (Wrong Speech in a Stone House) was copied by King Trần Anh Tông into the Tripitaka for circulation
- Đại hương hải ấn thi tập (The Book of Poetry Imprints of the Great Sea of Fragrant Water)
- Trần Nhân Tông thi tập (Trần Nhân Tông's Poetry Collection)
- Trung Hưng thực lục (2 volumes) Recording the Invasion of Yuan Invaders

According to the assessment in Lý Trần's poetry and literature book (volume 2) compiled by Nguyễn Huệ Chi, Trần Thị Băng Thanh, Đỗ Văn Hỷ và Trần Tú Châu, Trần Nhân Tông's poetry has the nature of "a smooth combination of philosophical and worldly sensibility, optimism, love of life, the altruistic heart of a great personality and delicate vibrations, the freedom-loving of an artist"[61] For example:

The country two times faced the invaders as the horse stained the mud

The river of country is stable for thousands of years.

(Xã tắc hai phen chồn ngựa đá

Non sông nghìn thuở vững âu vàng).[62]

Living amid Dust and Enjoying the Way

Living amid dust and enjoying
the way, you should let all things
take their course.
When hungry, just eat; when tired, just sleep.
The treasure is in your house; don't search any more.
Face the scenes, and have no thoughts;
then you don't need to ask for Zen.

Vietnamese: Cư trần lạc đạo phú
Ở đời vui đạo hãy tùy duyên,
Đói cứ ăn đi mệt ngủ liền.
Có báu trong nhà thôi tìm kiếm,
Vô tâm đối cảnh hỏi chi thiền.
(Translated into Vietnamese: Lê Mạnh Thát)[63]

61. https://vietbooks.info/threads/tho-van-ly-tran-tap-2-quyen-thuong-nxb- khoa-hoc-xa-hoi-1988-nguyen-hue-chi-965-trang.1740/

62. https://zingnews.vn/9-cau-noi-luu-danh-muon-doi-cua-de-vuong-danh- than-nuoc-viet-post873836.html

63. Toàn tập Trần Nhân Tông (Whole set on Trần Nhân Tông) Lê Mạnh

Confined in a breath, human life is short;
larger than two oceans of
gold, human greed is vast;
while being jailed in the palace of evil,
human suffers.
Blissful incomparably are those who enter the Buddha land.

Vietnamese:

Số đời một hơi thở Lòng người hai biển vàng
Cung ma dồn quá lắm Cõi Phật vui nào hơn.
(Translated into Vietnamese: Ven. Thích Thanh Từ)[64]

Leisure Time

I live in a serene place,
and see the mind
liberated.
The cool wind is seeping
through the shade of cypress
trees. Sitting on a Zen bed
beneath a tree,

Thát (In lần thứ 3 có sửa chữa bổ sung). Viện Nghiên Cứu Phật Học Việt Nam. NXB Phương Đông. 1999.

64. Trần Nhân Tông - Đức Vua Sáng Tổ Một Dòng Thiền (Trần Nhân Tông, The King Who Founded A Zen School). Translated and Commented by Nguyen Giac.https://thuvienhoasen.org/a11751/tran-nhan-tong-duc-vua-sang-to-mot-dong- thien-nguyen-giac

I read a sutra.
The two words "leisure time" are
more precious than ten thousand gold bars.

Vietnamese:

Cảnh vắng sống yên tự tại hồn,
Bóng tùng gió mát thổi
từng cơn.
Giường thiền một quyển kinh bên
gốc, Hai chữ thanh nhàn vạn nén
hơn.

(Translated into Vietnamese: Prof. Lê Mạnh Thát)[65]

Trần Nhân Tông King was a typical poet of the Trần Dynasty. His poetry has a special charm, not only of his lofty and profound ideas, but also because of the beauty that reaches the subtlety of words and expressions. He was considered a typical poet and cultural writer of Đại Việt in the medieval period. His name "Trần Nhân Tông" and "Trúc Lâm Thiền Sư" was given to many schools, associations, streets, cities, and provinces in Vietnam to remember the outstanding Zen Master and compassionate king.

The film, "Phật Hoàng Trần Nhân Tông" (Golden Buddha King Trần Nhân Tông) General director, meritorious artist Văn Lượng and his colleagues from Hải Phòng Television Studio (HFS) have begun pre-production of the forty-five-episode epic drama series, Phật Hoàng Trần Nhân Tông King .

With the enthusiasm of the production units and the contributions of cultural and historical researchers, it is

65. Như trên.

hoped that the film, The Golden Buddha Trần Nhân Tông, will be "an artistic work worthy of the stature of a prominent character in the history of the nation and the world."[66]

5.11. Death and Legacy

In 1307, when Pháp Loa was only twenty-four years old, Trúc Lâm wrote the mind verse and took the medicine bowl to pass on to Pháp Loa. On the first day of the Lunar New Year (1308), Trúc Lâm passed away. Trúc Lâm officially commissioned Pháp Loa to succeed the abbot of Siêu Loại Pagoda, the second ancestor of Trúc Lâm Buddhism. This happened in the wiT.N.ess of King Anh Tông.

Zen History narrated the moment the Trúc Lâm Master felt free entering the death state as below:

In the eighteenth day of the month, he walked to Tú Lâm Temple at An Kỳ Sanh Mountain. Feeling a headache, he said to two monks in the temple, "I want to hike to Ngọa Vân Peak, but my legs feel weak. What should I do?"

The two monks replied that they would help to carry him up. Coming to Ngọa Vân Temple at the peak, he said

66.https://nhandan.vn/bo-phim-su-thi-phat-hoang-tran-nhan-tong-post387865.html

thanks to the two monks, and urged them, "Go down the mountain and practice hard; don't play down the matter of birth and death."

In the nineteenth day of the month, he asked his attendant Pháp Không to go to Tử Tiêu Temple at Yên Tử Mountain and tell Bảo Sát to come down and see him urgently.

In the twenty-first day of the month, Bảo Sát arrived at Ngọa Vân Temple.

Trúc Lâm Master saw him and said, "I am departing now. Why do you come so late? If you still are unclear about Buddhist teachings, just ask me now."

Bảo Sát said, "When Mã Tổ felt ill, the head monk asked, 'Dear Master, how do you feel these days?' Mã Tổ replied, 'Sun Face Buddha, Moon Face Buddha.' What did that mean?"

Trúc Lâm Master spoke loudly, "The Three Sovereigns and Five Emperors-what were they?"

(A note should be made here. Sun Face Buddha and Moon Face Buddha are the names of two Buddhas whose faces look like a sun and a moon respectively. Both names are listed in the Ten Thousand Buddhas Sutra. It is said that Sun Face Buddha's life lasted 1,800 years, and Moon Face Buddha's life only one day and one night.)

Bảo Sát asked again, "What does the old saying 'As flowers bloom, so does the silk brocade; as bamboos in the south grow, so do the trees in the north' mean?"

Trúc Lâm Master replied, "They made you blind." Bảo Sát stopped asking.

Then the sky was dark and gloomy for several days.

The birds and monkeys in the forest cried sorrowfully.

In the night of the first day of the eleventh month of that year, the sky became clear and full of shining stars.

Trúc Lâm Master asked Bảo Sát, "What time is it now?"

Bảo Sát replied, "The hour of the mouse."

Trúc Lâm Master lifted the curtain, looked out and said, "Now is the time I have to go."

Bảo Sát asked, "Where are you going to?" Trúc Lâm

Master read the poem below.

If you constantly see that all things are unborn and that all things

are undying, all Buddhas appear constantly in front of your eyes. Nothing is coming or going.

Bảo Sát asked, "How about when it is unborn and undying?"

Trúc Lâm Master patted on Bao Sat's mouth, and said, "Don't talk in your sleep."

Trần Nhân Tông lay down on his right side as the Mahanirvana Buddha

This were the last minutes of a remarkable noble and royal character who devoted his life to the cause of the dhamma, country, and the people. After a fifteen-year reign, and Trần Nhân Tông lay down as a lion and passed away peacefully at the age of fifty- one, in the year 1308.

Trúc Lâm Master lived only half a century; however, the Zen school he founded has become now the largest one in Vietnam, specially with the support of the Great Zen Master Thích Thanh Từ of the twentieth and twenty-first century.

When Trần Nhân Tông passed away, the court and the people mourned and resounded throughout the world. One historian commented, "There are few kings in the nation's history that are fully recorded about the admiration of the people after their death..."[67]

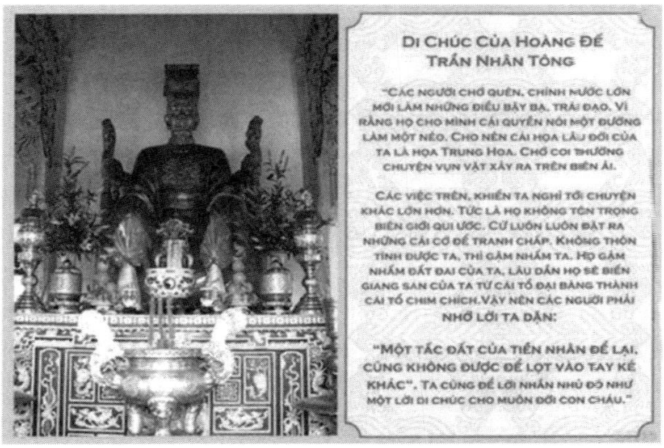

Pháp Loa obeyed his master's will, performed the cremation ceremony, and collected pieces of five-color bony relics. King Trần Anh Tông built a stupa in the court of Vàm Yên Temple on Yên Tử Mountain. The king named the stupa, "Đại Thánh Trần Triều Trúc Lâm Đầu Đà Tĩnh Tuệ Giác Hoàng Điều Ngự Tổ Phật."[68]

---

67. https://nhandan.vn/bo-phim-su-thi-phat-hoang-tran-nhan-tong-post387865.html

68. Lê Văn Hưu, Phan Phu Tiên, Ngô Sĩ Liên. 1993. 193.

One part of Trần Nhân Tông's relics worshipped at Huệ Quang Stupa

The statue of King Giác Hoàng Trần Nhân Tông in Huệ Quang Stupa

VI. COMPARISON OF THE GREAT.N.ESS BETWEEN KING ASHOKA AND KING TRẦN NHÂN TÔNG

Like Emperor Ashoka, Trần Nhân Tông King traveled all over the country to encourage his people to lead a spiritual life. He also taught ten good deeds for their prosperity.

Now that we have discussed the differences and matters related to the subject, we look into the similarities between the two great emperors.

Both emperors belonged to powerful dynasties from India and Vietnam-Ashoka the Great from the Maurya Dynasty and Emperor Trần Nhân Tông King from the Trần Dynasty.[69]

The reigning period of Dharmassoka was a glorious time of Buddhism in religiously awake India, and in Vietnam as well during the reigning days of King Trần Nhân Tông.

When we go through the life stories of both Ashoka and Trần Nhân Tông, we find both had immense love and affection towards mankind and their fellow living beings and also for Buddhism, despite its sectors or chapters.[70]

The similarity between the two kings is clear when we look into the wars they faced or launched. Emperor Ashoka waged war to expand his kingdom and to create an unchallenged sovereignty. Trần Nhân Tông King waged war to protect his country, citizens, and culture from Mongolian invaders.

However, both had seen the bloodshed with their own eyes and learned lessons. According to historians, millions died as a result of those wars while property in some areas

69. Lê Văn Hưu, Phan Phu Tiên, Ngô Sĩ Liên. 1993. 192.

70. Ibid.

was fully destroyed. Both kings devoted their royal power to spread Buddhism and to perform beneficial activities among Maha Sangha and their beloved subjects.

It is said that Trần Nhân Tông King did not consume fish or meat. Emperor Ashoka, in this regard, proceeding further, prohibited slaughter of animals all over the country. On the other hand, according to their lifestyles, both were brave and had enough courage to face and handle any situation. They both worked with no limit to serve the people for the betterment of their lives.

It seems both may have faced challenges when they were propagating Buddhism as there were other people following different traditional beliefs. When Emperor Ashoka made Buddhism a world religion, Emperor Trần Nhân Tông made the Trúc Lâm Zen sector of Buddhism strong and powerful in his empire throughout the territory of Vietnam, and the countries where Vietnamese residents live and throughout until the 21st century.

VII. THE GREAT CONTRIBUTION FOR WORLD PEACE AND SOCIAL HARMONY

Both Emperor Ashoka of India and Emperor Trần Nhân Tông of Vietnam made great contributions for world peace and social harmony for their countries and human beings.

From a murderous and ferocious king, Ashoka became awakened as he saw the bloody river from his conquest of Kalinga on the east coast. Since then, he became an honest gentle follower of the Buddha whose dharma advocates compassion, wisdom and especially non-violence, not injuring others physically or mentally.

Looking at the history of Buddhism is the seeing the history of altruism, sacrifice, care for people, helping people to overcome suffering, live peacefully and happily in the present and future. Therefore, the king used the dharma of the Blessed One to rule the country such as:

7.1. Ten precepts:

- Not to kill or encourage others to kill.
- Not to steal or encourage others to steal.
- Not to engage in licentious acts or encourage others to do so. A monk is expected to abstain from sexual conduct entirely.
- Not to use false words and speech or encourage others to do so.
- Not to trade or sell alcoholic beverages or encourage others to do so.
- Not to broadcast the misdeeds or faults of the Buddhist assembly, nor encourage others to do so.
- Not to praise oneself and speak ill of others or encourage others to do so.
- Not to be stingy or encourage others to do so.
- Not to harbor anger or encourage others to be angry.
- Not to speak ill of the Buddha, the dharma or the sangha (lit. the Triple Jewel) or encourage others to do so.

Citizens and Buddhists keep the precepts to avoid bad cause- effects and to increase good deeds, providing a safe and happy environment for the individual, family and community.

7. 2. Six Harmonious Disciplines

- Harmony in having the same viewpoints
- Hrmony in observing the same precepts

- Harmony in living together
- Harmony in speaking without conflict
- Harmony in experiencing Dharma bliss
- Harmony in sharing benefits.

The six ways of harmony help to connect individuals as a whole who can co-live, co-work, co-share and co-progress on the spiritual path. The country is strong thanks to the harmony of each person, each family, and community. The Ten Precepts and the Six Harmonious Disciplines are a good force for world peace and social harmony.

King Ashoka had these teachings engraved on stone pillars as a decree of maintaining harmony and peace. He ordered the Buddhist missions to bring these happy and liberated messages outside the Indian border, to Ceylon, Thailand, Laos, China,

Vietnam and so on. For example, the king sent his son, the crown prince aka Bhikkhu Mahinda (Mahendra) to Ceylon to establish Buddhism and later he sent his daughter, the Princess Sanghamitra to go Ceylon to ordain nuns and spread the right way to liberation.

In addition, King Asoka was a benefactor who supported the very large sangha by providing financial and food support regularly. To keep the pure sangha, any monk who pretended to infiltrate the sangha, who does not really practice will be severely punished. King Asoka also played the role of a powerful protector who strengthened Buddhism. The king also built many pagodas and erected towers in many states of ancient India.Today the archaeological foundations are still eloquently presented.

Ashoka was the king who was first credited with spreading the Buddha's message of nonviolence, compassion, and wisdom out of India. Buddhism is a way of living peacefully, happily, mindfully and awake. This method has the ability to reforce the transformation of society into an orderly, safe, just, peaceful and happy place. This method has been accepted, existed, and integrated in many countries regardless of the national origin, marital status, ethnicity, color, gender, race, age and occupation. Buddhism can be vividly in harmony with other cultures, religions, philosophies, and organizations to jointly reinforce a liberated world worth living.

As with Emperor Asoka, Trần Nhân Tông King took the Ten Precepts, Six Harmonious Disciplines and studied the Zen philosophy of Buddhism as the main thought to build the Buddhist- based society. He led his citizens and Buddhist disciples to cultivate wisdom and virtue, unite people's hearts, protect the country from foreign invaders, and build a peaceful state.

When the country was unsafe by aggression, Trần Nhân Tông King put aside his spiritual practice to defend his country to protect the state. He governed the country keeping the people safe, and expressed the spirit of national self-reliance, which will be remembered forever.

When the country was at peace, he focused on education, selection of a Mandarin system, building a state apparatus with integrity, so that the society would be just, equal, and developed. When his son was mature enough to run the kingdom, he yielded the throne to him and become a monk who lived a simple and ascetic life to search for the truth on a remote mountain. He became enlightened and shared the way of awakening (the Trúc Lâm Zen School) to all which are still well illustrated by his poems, edicts, and works in the Trần Dynasty.

With the wisdom and profound vision of a Zen Master, he understood that Buddhist teachings are the place to relieve suffering and save lives, help sentient beings give up evil, do good and live purely. Being a king must be ethical for the sake of sentient beings. He built a good model to bring harmony in the sangha, royalty, and society for his citizens and Buddhist disciples. He applied the practice of the six Buddhist Harmonious Rules to build a peaceful and prosperous Đại Việt country.

Firstly, in terms of diplomacy, he attempted to build a close friendship with the neighboring country located on the southern border, Champa. To tighten the diplomatic relationship that had good momentum, to discourage the Đại Việt people from the looting of their Champa neighbors and increase the peacekeeping, Trần Nhân Tông King sent his daughter, Princess Huyền Trân, to Champa to marry King Che Man. In regard to the wedding betrothal of the bride, King Chế Mân offered the two provinces of Châu Ô and Châu Lý (the present is Thuận Châu and Hóa Châu of Vietnam)[71]. Ever since, both countries have been friends with a connection. This peace and harmony extended to the surrounding areas.

Secondly, in order to consolidate the long-term peace, he released prisoners of the Mongolian-Yuan that the army captured in the three wars to create favorable conditions for relations between the two countries, a wise and flexible decision in Đại Việt's foreign policy at that time. Perhaps that is why Trần Nhân Tông is considered by the world as the most representative of the spirit of social reconciliation and world peace.

VIII. CONLCUSION

In the history of the nation and Buddhism, Ashoka and Trần Nhân Tông were outstanding emperors in India and Vietnam. They advocated bringing Buddhism into the world, actively spreading it among the people, promoting the spirit of harmony among hundreds of families, building and fostering independence, self-reliance, and harmony in the world, harmony between king-prince,

71. https://sdl.thuathienhue.gov.vn/?gd=20&cn=1&id=232&tc=4165

harmony between father-son, harmony between husband-wife, family, and the nation. That thought is the root of the nation's lasting strength, and over time has become a tradition of the nation. They created a civilized and good Buddhist-based society for themselves and for the global community. Indeed, Emperor Ashoka and Trần Nhân Tông King were keepers of world peace and social harmony and "*only the victory of Dharma is truly a supreme victory; Thanks to that victory, everyone can live peacefully.*" (Emperor Ashoka)[72]

The lives of both emperors are an invaluable legacy for posterity. They have become international figures who are the source of inspiration for future generations.

Kolkata, July 2, 2023

Ven. Dr. Bhikṣuṇī T.N. Gioi Huong
huongsentemple@gmail.com

72. Thich Nguyên Tạng. Một ông vua hộ trì Phật Pháp. 09/09/2015. https://thuvienhoasen.org/a23735/dai-de-a-duc-mot-ong-vua-ho-tri-phat-phap

SỰ ĐÓNG GÓP CHO HÒA BÌNH THẾ GIỚI VÀ AN TOÀN XÃ HỘI CỦA HOÀNG ĐẾ A-DỤC VÀ VUA TRẦN NHÂN TÔNG

Ni Sư TS.T.N.. Giới Hương
tại Hội nghị của Siddharth United Social Welfare Mission, Kolkata, Ấn Độ, ngày 02 tháng 07 năm 2023

Để bắt đầu, có thể nói đây là thời điểm thích hợp để ghi lại đôi dòng về lịch sử Đức Phật, Phật giáo và nền tảng tôn giáo của Ấn Độ và Việt Nam trước khi đi đến chủ đề đáng quan tâm, "Sự đóng góp vĩ đại cho hòa bình thế giới và hòa hợp xã hội của Hoàng đế Ashoka của Ấn Độ và Hoàng đế Trần Nhân Tông của

Việt Nam".

Từ nhiều thế kỷ, Ấn Độ và Việt Nam đã duy trì mối quan hệ truyền thống, đặc biệt là trong lĩnh vực văn hóa, tôn giáo cùng với chính trị, thương mại và kinh tế, vv... Cả hai quốc gia đều tôn trọng và vinh danh các nhà lãnh đạo tôn giáo quốc gia của nhau.

I. ĐỨC PHẬT THÍCH CA MÂU NI Ở ẤN ĐỘ

Bản đồ nước Ấn độ (Google)[73]

Trong vài thế kỷ trước Công nguyên, nền văn minh của Ấn Độ được chia thành mười sáu vương quốc, tám trong số đó là các vương quốc phần còn lại là các nước cộng hòa. Trong số những vương quốc đó, hùng mạnh nhất là nước Magadha và Kosala."Nước cộng hòa Sakya nhỏ bé được cai trị bởi vua xứ Kosala, vị vua được triều cống. Đất nước Sakyas thuộc Triều đại Kshatriya Solar còn

73. https://www.buddhisttour.com/map.html

được gọi là "eslverajas" hay "các vị vua."[74] Vào giữa thế kỷ này, thủ lĩnh của họ là Vua Tịnh Phạn (Suddhodana), có kinh đô tại thành Ca-tỳ-la-vệ (Kapilawastu). Vào năm 623 trước Công nguyên, hoàng hậu Maha Maya đang đi từ thành Kapilavastu về nhà cha mẹ ruột ở Devdaha để sinh đứa con đầu lòng. Trên đường đi, hoàng hậu hạ sinh một thiên tử dưới tán cây hoa Vô Ưu tại vườn Lâm-tỳ-ni (Lumbini) xinh đẹp.

Một vị ẩn sĩ tên Asita đã đến thăm vua Suddhodana và tiên đoán rằng một ngày nào đó thái tử, con của Đức vua sẽ trở thành vị cứu tinh của nhân loại. Sau đó, Thái tử được đặt tên là Sĩ-Đạt-Đa (Siddhartha) được vua cha cung cấp mọi sự bảo vệ đầy đủ tiện nghi cuộc sống xa hoa nhung lụa. Khi thái tử Sĩ-Đạt-Đa còn trẻ, vua cha Tịnh Phạn đã sắp xếp cho Ngài kết hôn với vị công chúa xinh đẹp nước láng giềng tên là Da-du-đà-la (Yasodhara). Họ có một đứa con trai tên là Rahula. Tuy nhiên, ngay cả trước khi kết hôn, thái tử Sĩ-Đạt-Đa đã có một mong muốn mạnh mẽ từ bỏ cuộc sống thế gian để sống đời tu phạm hạnh nhưng cha của Ngài đã ngăn cản điều đó. Sau khi sinh con trai, thái tử Sĩ-Đạt-Đa nghĩ rằng con trai mình sẽ là một trở ngại cho những ý nguyện tương lai của mình. Một ngày nọ, Thái tử quyết định rời bỏ cuộc sống xa hoa trần tục này trong lúc đó, khi vợ và con trai đang ngủ, Ngài đã rời khỏi cung điện mà không một ai để ý.

Trên cỗ xe ngựa của mình, thái tử Sĩ-Đạt-Đa đã băng qua một khu rừng. Sau đó, Ngài trút bỏ hoàng bào, dùng kiếm cắt mái tóc dài của mình trở thành một nhà tu khổ hạnh. Ngài đi tìm những người thầy có thể dạy cho Ngài chân lý của cuộc sống. Ngài tiếp thu tất cả những gì các vị thầy đã dạy, nhưng khao khát chân lý của Ngài vẫn chưa được giải đáp không nguôi ngoai trong lòng. Ngài tiếp tục đi tìm, cuối cùng đến một vùng đất với ấn tượng bởi phong cảnh thiên nhiên tươi đẹp, nơi mà hiện nay được

74. P.V. Bapat, 2500 Years of Buddhism (New Delhi, Department of Information, Government of India, 1959), 1–7.

biết đến gọi là Bồ-đề-đạo tràng (Bodhgaya, Bihar, Ấn độ).

Lúc đó Bồ tát Cồ Đàm (tức thái tử Sĩ-Đạt-Đa) nghe nói rằng muốn giải thoát phải thực hành khổ hạnh khắc nghiệt, Ngài đã trải nghiệm các hình thức tự hành hạ bản thân khác nhau trong sáu năm. Do đó, cơ thể Ngài ốm đi chỉ còn da bọc xương như một bộ xương biết đi. Ở giai đoạn này, Ngài nhận ra rằng sự hành hạ thể xác không phải là cách để đạt được giác ngộ nên đã quyết định dùng lại thực phẩm.

Bồ tát Gotama thiền định trên sông Niranjana

Sau khi thọ thực một bát cháo sữa do nàng Sujata, con gái của một gia đình thương gia cúng dường, Ngài dần hồi lấy lại sức khỏe tốt hơn. Sau đó, Ngài nỗ lực tập trung vào tâm trí đạt đến sự an tịnh giải thoát. Ngài giác ngộ dưới cội cây bồ đề thành Phật hiệu là Thích Ca Mâu Ni và cây này được gọi là Sri Maha Bodhi (cây Bồ-đề thiêng). Do vậy, Đức Phật là người đã "*trải nghiệm, hiểu cách thoát khổ đau và chia sẻ phương pháp ấy cho nhân loại.*"[75]

75. V.D. Chand Mahajan and Co., Ancient India (New Delhi: Ram Nagar), 295–298.

Trong lịch sử các tôn giáo Ấn Độ, Phật giáo chiếm một vị trí độc tôn, trước hết là mở ra những cánh cửa của sự giải thoát tu tập không chỉ cho người Ấn Độ mà còn cho tất cả các thành phần xã hội trên thế giới. Từ đầu, Phật giáo luôn dựa trên nền tảng "*hòa bình, khoan dung, bất bạo động và đoàn kết như một liên tôn giáo thế giới.*"[76]

II. CÁC VỊ VUA VÀ HOÀNG ĐẾ TRONG THỜI ĐỨC PHẬT

Trong suốt cuộc đời của Đức Phật Thích Ca Mâu Ni, Ngài đã nhận được sự bảo trợ của hoàng gia từ các vị vua chúa hùng mạnh và các hoàng hậu của thời kỳ này.

Vua Bình-sa vương (Bimbisara) xứ Ma-kiệt-dà (Magadha) là người đầu tiên cúng dường cho Đức Phật một ngôi tinh xá để trú ngụ. Hoàng hậu của Vua Bình-sa vương là Khema, trở thành một Phật tử thuần thành. Sau khi, Đức Phật diệt độ, Thái tử A-xà-thế (Ajasatta), con trai của vua Bình-sa vương, tổ chức Cuộc kiết tập Phật giáo đầu tiên (sangayana)" tại thành Vương Xá (Rajgir).[77] Vua Prasanjith Kosala của Sravasti (Uttar Pradesh ngày nay) là một người bảo trợ Phật giáo. Chính tại Sravasti, Đức Phật đã trải qua hầu hết các mùa an cư kiết hạ (Vassana). Những sắc dân Bắc Ấn Lichchavis của Cộng hòa Lichchavis (ngày nay là bang Bihar) là những đệ tử của Đức Phật và Đức Phật đã tổ chức lại bảy luật bất tùy thuộc của họ để được đưa vào trật tự của Phật giáo.

Ở Kosambi dưới sự cai trị của Vua Udeni, cuộc tranh cãi đầu tiên xảy ra giữa các Tỳ kheo. Họ chia thành hai phần-pháp và Luật.

76. Maha Thera Dharmapal, Ashoka–2300 (Kolkata, India: The Bengal Buddhist Association, 1997), 15, 121, 178.

77. Ven. Dr. Medhankara Maha Thero, The Great Buddhist Emperors of Asia (Bhoomi Prakashan. Nagpur, Maharashrtra, India, 1959), 1, 41, 56, 72, 93, 100, 110, 128, 134, 146, 169, 195, 222, 234, 246, 272.

Không ai có thể quên vua Suddodana của Kapilawattu, cha của Đức Phật. Ngài đã hết lòng hỗ trợ và tôn kính Đức Phật đến cuối đời. Bên cạnh Hoàng đế A-dục Aśoka), còn có những nhà cai trị vĩ đại bảo trợ Đức Phật và Phật giáo theo nhiều phương cách khác nhau. Họ đã truyền bá đạo Phật ở nhiều đất nước khác nhau trên thế giới như: Vua Dharmaraj Milinda (*khoảng năm 175 TCN*), Hoàng đế Kanishka (*78–101 hoặc 120 sau Công nguyên*), và Hoàng đế Harshawardhana (*425 sau Công nguyên*).

Vua Ansuverma của Nepal (*thế kỷ thứ bảy sau Công Nguyên*), Hoàng đế Tsrong Tsang Gampo của Tây Tạng (*năm 617*), Hoàng đế Yu Tee của nhà Lương Trung Quốc (*năm 502– 549*), Vua Wang Kiyen của Triều Tiên (*năm 1340*), Shoroku, được gọi là DharmAśoka Nhật Bản (*năm 580*), Dhamma Cheti của Miến Điện (*năm 1476*), Hoàng đế Dutugamunu của Sri Lanka (*101–77 TCN*), Maha Parakramabahu của Sri Lanka (*1153–1186*), Hoàng đế Hốt Tất Liệt của Mông Cổ (*năm 1254*), Sri Suryawansam của Siam (*Thái Lan, năm 1355*), Jayaverma của Campodia (Campuchia *năm* 1*182– 1202*), Vua Fanewn của Lào (*năm 1353*), Vua Indra Verma II của Vương quốc Champa, Việt Nam ngày nay (*năm 860– 890*), và Sri Vijayaag là những nhà cai trị khác đã truyền bá Phật giáo ở các quốc gia nói trên."[78]

III. HOÀNG ĐẾ A-DỤC

Vua A-dục (Aśoka, Asoka, Ashoka) một hoàng đế Ấn Độ của triều đại Ma-Kiệt-Đà (Maurya), người đã cai trị gần như toàn bộ tiểu lục địa Ấn Độ từ 268 đến 232 trước Công Nguyên, là một trong những hoàng đế vĩ đại nhất của Ấn Độ. Vua A-dục trị vì một vương quốc trải dài từ dãy núi Hindu Kush ở Afghanistan đến bang Bangladesh hiện đại ở phía Đông. Nó bao phủ toàn bộ tiểu lục địa Ấn

78. P.V. Bapat, 2500 Years of Buddhism (India: Bapat Ministry of Information and Broadcasting, Government of India, 1959), 50, 53, 56.

Độ ngoại trừ một phần của Tamil Nadu và Kerala ngày nay. Thủ đô của đế chế là Pataliputra (ở Magadha, Bihar ngày nay), với các tỉnh lỵ tại Taxila và Ujjain.

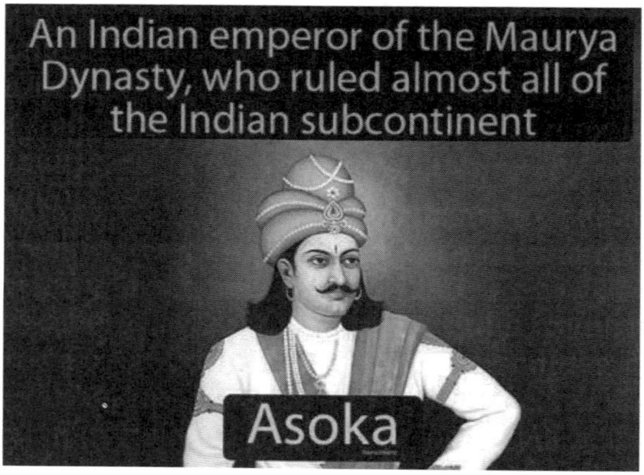

Khoảng năm 260 trước Công Nguyên, Vua A-dục đã tiến hành một cuộc chiến tàn khốc ác liệt chống lại nhà nước Kalinga (Orissa ngày nay). Khi chứng kiến những cái chết hàng loạt trong trận chiến Kalinga, mà chính ông đã tiến hành vì ham muốn để chinh phục, đã dẫn đến hơn 100.000 người chết và 150.000 người bị trục xuất, chiến trường xảy ra khiến dòng sông đầy máu đỏ của dân thường vô tội.

Từ đó, Vua A-dục hối hận tìm đến giáo lý tình thương và trí tuệ của Phật giáo bắt đầu từ khoảng năm 263 trước Công Nguyên. Sau đó, Vua chuyên tâm vào việc truyền bá Phật giáo trên khắp châu Á, thành lập các di tích đánh dấu một số địa điểm quan trọng trong cuộc đời của Đức Phật Cồ Đàm. Vua A-dục coi Phật giáo là một học thuyết có thể làm nền tảng văn hóa cho sự thống nhất về chính trị. Vua A-dục còn được biết đến như Phật tử hào hiệp cúng dường rộng rãi cho tam bảo một nhà từ thiện bố thí cho dân nghèo. Ở Kalinga, trong sắc lệnh Vua thường gọi người dân của mình là 'con ruột', và đề cập mình với tư cách là một người cha, luôn mong muốn con sống an vui hạnh phúc.

Trong tiếng Phạn "Aśoka" có nghĩa là; "không đau, không buồn". Trong các sắc lệnh triều đình, Vua được gọi là Devānāmpriya (*Pali: Devānaṃpiya nghĩa là Người được các vị thần yêu quý*), và Priyadarśin (Pali: Piyadasī nghĩa là Người quan tâm đến người khác). Sự yêu mến của vua được ví như "cây Saraca asoca, hay cây Ashoka"[79] cũng được đề cập đến trong Ashokavadana.

Trong cuốn sách "*The Outline of History,*" tác giả H.G. Wells đã viết về Vua A-dục như sau: "Giữa hàng vạn các vị vua đã đi vào lịch sử, sự uy nghiêm và ân sủng của họ, sự thanh nhã của các hoàng thân và những đạo hạnh tương tự, tên của Vua A-dục tỏa sáng rạng ngời nổi bật gần như một mình là một ngôi sao." Trong *Mahavamsa (*Đại Biên Niên Sử) Sri Lanka và *một phần của Divyavadana* có tường thuật về Vua Pháp A-dục. Quốc huy của nước Cộng hòa Ấn Độ hiện đại là sự phóng tác từ trụ đá bốn con sư tử của Vua A-dục. Dhammachakka hay bánh xe Dhamma cũng được mô tả ở Quốc kỳ Ấn Độ. Đó là những gì Vua A Dục đã cống hiến, hiện còn cho đến thế kỷ XXI ngày nay

3.1. Cuộc đời của Đại đế A-dục

Vua A-dục được sinh ra bởi cha là Hoàng đế Mauryan, Bindusara, và mẫu hậu Dharmā (hay Dhamma). Asoka là cháu trai của Chandragupta Maurya, người sáng lập Vương triều Maurya. Các văn bản Avadana đề cập rằng mẹ của ông là Hoàng hậu Subhadrangī. Theo Ashokavadana, bà ấy là con gái của một Bà-la-môn đến từ thành phố Champa.

Phẩm chất hiếu chiến, háo thắng của Vua A-dục đã bộc lộ ngay từ nhỏ và lớn lên được huấn luyện trong quân đội hoàng gia "*Bởi vốn nổi tiếng là một chiến binh đáng sợ và là một vị tướng tàn nhẫn, nên được phái đi để kiềm chế*

79. D.R. Bhandarakar, Aśoka (Calcutta: Calcutta University Press, 1969), 166, 230

"bạo loạn ở tỉnh Avanti của đế chế Maurya."[80]

Sử Phật giáo *Divyavadana* mô tả Vua A-dục đã từng dập tắt một cuộc nổi dậy của các bộ trưởng ác độc gây nên. Đây có thể xảy ra dưới thời của Bindusara. Theo lời kể của Taranatha rằng Chanakya, vị cố vấn trưởng của hoàng đế Bindusara, đã tiêu diệt các quý tộc và chư hầu của mười sáu thị trấn biến mình thành chúa tể của tất cả các lãnh thổ giữa biển Đông và biển Tây. Một số nhà sử học xem đây là dấu hiệu của cuộc chinh phục Deccan của Bindusara, trong khi những người khác coi đó là sự đàn áp một cuộc nổi dậy. Tiếp theo đó, Vua A-dục đóng quân tại Ujjayini với tư cách là thống đốc. Cái chết của Bindusara vào năm 272 trước Công nguyên đã dẫn đến một cuộc chiến tranh giành kế vị. Sau khi lên ngôi, Vua A-dục đã mở rộng đế chế của mình trong tám năm liên tiếp.

3.2. Chinh phục Kalinga

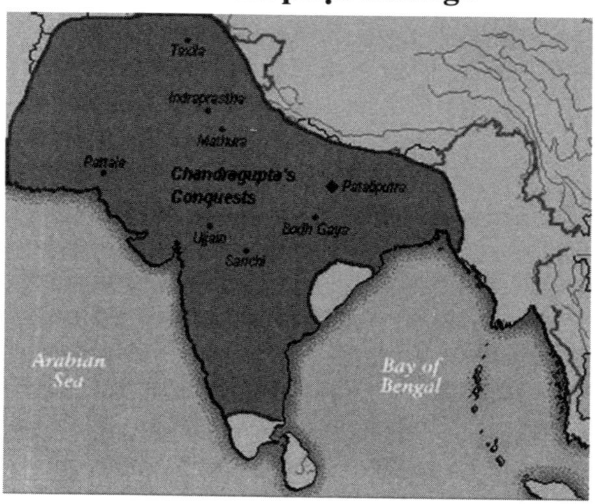

Kalinga (tiếp giáp với Vịnh Bengal) và Đế chế Maurya (màu xanh) trước cuộc tấn công của Đại đế A-dục

80. G.M. Bongard-Levin, Mauryan India (India: Stosius, 1986), 186.

Trong khi phần đầu cuộc đời của Vua A-dục rõ ràng khá tàn bạo hiếu sát, tuy nhiên sau đó vua đã trở thành một Phật tử thuần thành của Đức Phật sau cuộc chinh phục Kalinga trên bờ biển phía Đông của Ấn Độ ngày nay là bang Orissa và North Coastal Andhra Pradesh. Kalinga là một quốc gia tự hào về chủ quyền và dân chủ.

Với nền dân chủ nghị viện quân chủ, đó là một ngoại lệ ở Bharata cổ đại, nơi tồn tại khái niệm "*Rajdharma*" hay "nhiệm vụ của những người cai trị," về bản chất đã gắn liền với khái niệm về lòng dũng cảm và pháp luật. Ở Kalinga, chiến tranh đã xảy ra tám năm sau khi Đại đế A-dục đăng quang. Từ bản khắc thứ mười ba của vua, chúng ta biết rằng Kalinga là một trận chiến lớn và gây ra cái chết của hơn 100.000 binh sĩ và nhiều những người dân phòng thủ; hơn 150.000 người đã bị trục xuất. Khi vua đi bộ qua dòng sông Kalinga sau cuộc chinh phục của mình, "để vui mừng trước chiến thắng của mình, Vua đã bị xúc động bởi số lượng thi thể nằm rải rác ở bờ sông và tiếng than khóc của tang quyến vang rền khắp nơi".[81]

81. D.C. Aher, Ashoka the Great (Delhi: B.R. Publishers, 1995), 226, 228. https://en.wikipedia.org/wiki/Kalinga_War

3.3. Sự chuyển hóa theo Phật giáo

Đại đế A-dục cảm thấy hối hận trước cuộc chinh phục Kalinga trong quá trình xâm lăng này, đất nước chưa từng bị chinh phục trước đây giờ đã bị tàn sát, chết chóc và bắt cóc xảy ra,khắp nơi, vua cảm thấy đau buồn và hối tiếc sâu sắc, Vua hiểu rằng bạn bè và gia đình của người quá cố sẽ còn đau khổ hơn nhiều. Truyền thuyết kể rằng một ngày sau khi trận chiến kết thúc, Đại đế A-dục mạo hiểm ra ngoài dạo chơi thành phố và tất cả những gì vua có thể thấy là những ngôi nhà bị cháy và xác chết nằm la liệt.

Cuộc chiến chết chóc với Kalinga đã biến Hoàng đế A-dục đầy thù hận thành một hoàng đế có sự bình tĩnh, ổn định, chánh niệm, từ bi và hòa bình. Vua trở thành người Phật tử bảo trợ cho Phật giáo. Theo nhà Ấn Độ học lỗi lạc, A. L.Basham, tôn giáo cá nhân của Đại đế A-dục là Phật giáo, nếu không phải trước đó, thì chắc chắn là sau chiến tranh Kalinga. Tuy nhiên, theo ông Basham, Giáo Pháp do vua A Dục chính thức truyền bá không phải tất cả là của Phật giáo. Tuy nhiên, sự bảo trợ của Ông đã dẫn đến sự phát triển của Phật giáo ở đế chế Mauryan và các vương quốc khác trong thời kỳ cai trị của vua và trên toàn thế giới từ khoảng năm 250 trước Công Nguyên

Một điểm nổi bật khác trong sự nghiệp của Đại đế A-dục, con trai là hoàng tử Mahinda (Mahendra) và con gái là công chúa Sanghamitra (tên có nghĩa là "người bạn của Tăng đoàn", người đã thành lập Phật giáo ở Ceylon (nay là Sri Lanka). Thông tin về cuộc đời và triều đại của Đại đế A-dục chủ yếu đến từ một số lượng tương đối nhỏ của các bản kinh gốc Phật giáo. Đặc biệt, bản tiếng Phạn (Sanskrit) *Ashokavadana* (*Truyện về Ashoka*), được viết vào thế kỷ thứ hai, và hai bộ biên niên sử Pāli của Sri Lanka (Dipavamsa và Mahavamsa), cung cấp hầu hết các thông tin hiện được biết về Đại đế A-dục. Thông tin bổ sung được đóng góp bởi các sắc lệnh của Đại đế A-dục, người được cho là tác giả cuối cùng được quy cho Đại đế A-dục trong truyền thuyết Phật giáo sau phát hiện ra các danh sách triều đại đã đưa ra tên được sử dụng trong các sắc lệnh (Priyadarshi: 'Người coi trọng tất cả mọi người với tình cảm') như một tiêu đề hoặc tên bổ sung cho Ashoka *Maurya. Di tích kiến trúc thời kỳ của Ông đã được tìm thấy tại "Kumhrar, PaT.N.a, bao gồm một tu viện cổ đại với tám mươi cây cột.*"[82]

Đại đế A-dục đã thực sự thú nhận ngừng digvijaya (chinh phục bằng bạo lực) và tìm kiếm dhammavijaya (chinh phục bằng giáo Pháp). Vua cai trị đất nước của mình bằng Phật pháp với nhiều việc thiện. Triều đại của vua trở nên nhân đạo hơn khi cai trị theo Phật pháp. Ngài là vị vua đầu tiên cho xây dựng các đạo dụ Phật giáo lớn có khắc

82. Sulochana Ayyar, Costume and Ornaments as Depicted in the Early Sculptures of Gwarlior Museum), 186

chữ trên khắp Ấn Độ và Trung Á. Vua thành lập một bộ phận Phật giáo để xem xét việc giáo dục đạo đức cho Tăng đoàn và người dân. Vua đã đi dhammayatra (hành hương) đến những nơi linh thiêng và thành tâm cúng dường rộng rãi các vật dụng cần thiết cho Tăng đoàn. Vua đã tuyên bố với những các nước láng giềng của mình rằng Ngài không có ý định bành trướng đối với các quốc gia giáp với đế chế của mình. Sau khi kỳ kết tập kinh điển lần thứ ba hoàn thành, việc truyền bá giáo pháp đến chín quốc gia lân cận đã chứng kiến sự lan rộng của Phật giáo Nguyên thủy dưới sự bảo trợ của Đại đế A-dục như sau: "*Chín quốc gia là Kashmir và Gandhara (N. Punjab), Mahisamandala (phía Nam dãy núi Vindhyan), Vanavasi (N. Kanara), Aparantaka (N. Gujarat, Kathiawar, Kacch và Sind), Maharattha (quốc gia của người Marathi, Bombay hiện đại), các quốc gia Yona (các chủng tộc ngoại lai ở biên giới Tây Bắc, vương quốc Hy Lạp-Bactria), Himavanta (vùng Himalaya), Suvannabhumi (Hạ Myanmar, Thái Lan, Java, và thậm chí cả Malaya) và Tambapanni (Sri Lanka)*, v.v."[83]

Vua A-dục đã dành rất nhiều tiền bạc để phát triển nền giáo dục Phật giáo, xây dựng các tu viện, tháp, cột trụ, vv…. Ngài cũng xây dựng đại bảo tháp Sanchi và dựng lên hàng ngàn tháp Phật giáo để thờ xá lợi của Đức Phật. Vua đã xây dựng tịnh xá cho các nhà sư và tịnh xá nổi tiếng ở Pataliputra được đặt theo tên của vua là "*Aśokarama*". Vua cũng giúp phát triển các tịnh xá (Trung tâm Đào tạo Tri thức) như ở Nalanda và Taxila, ngoài việc xây dựng tháp Sanchi và Mahabodhi. Vua là một người hỗ trợ tuyệt vời cho sự nghiệp hoằng truyềnTam Bảo lan rộng khỏi biên giới Ấn Độ.

3.4. Vua A Dục là nhà chiêm bái Phật tích đầu tiên

Đại đế A-dục là một trong những nhà chiêm bái Phật

83. http://www.suttas.com/king-Aśoka.html

tích Ấn Độ đầu tiên, là người có công để lại những dấu vết của Phật giáo cổ đại cho ngày nay qua các công trình xây dựng, bia ký, cột trụ, tu viện, chùa tháp.

Vào năm thứ 20 của triều đại, Vua A Dục đã cầu thỉnh Ngài Ưu Ba Cúc Đa đưa đi chiêm bái hết tất cả những Phật tích tại Ấn Độ. Vua A Dục cùng với hoàng gia Khổng Tước dưới sự hướng dẫn của Ngài Ưu Ba Cúc Đa đã thực hiện chuyến đi chiêm bái này trong vòng 265 ngày để đến tận nơi và chiêm bái tất cả những thánh tích tại Ấn Độ, từ Lâm Tỳ Ni cho đến Câu Thi Na, tại mỗi thánh tích vua A Dục đều cho xây dựng bảo tháp, bia đá và trụ đá để đánh dấu nơi mà Đức Phật đã từng lưu trú và thuyết giảng lúc còn tại thế. Chính nhờ những trụ đá, bia đá này mà ngày nay hàng đệ tử Phật mới biết chính xác về các Phật tích.[84]

3.5. Sắc lệnh của Đại đế A-dục

Các Sắc lệnh của Vua A-dục là một bộ sưu tập gồm ba mươi ba bản khắc trên Trụ đá của Ngài, cũng như trên những tảng đá và vách hang được xây dưới triều đại của Vua. Những dòng chữ này được truyền khắp Pakistan và Ấn Độ ngày nay (bỏ:và) đại diện cho bằng chứng hữu hình đầu tiên của Phật giáo. Các sắc lệnh mô tả chi tiết sự phát triển rộng rãi đầu tiên của Phật giáo thông qua sự bảo trợ của một trong những vị vua hùng mạnh nhất trong lịch sử Ấn Độ, cung cấp thêm thông tin về "*sự cải đạo của Đại đế A-dục, đạo đức, giới luật thiền môn, và quan niệm của* Đại đế A-dục *về phúc lợi xã hội và loài động vật*".[85]

Những lời tuyên bố của Đại đế A-dục được khắc trên những tảng đá ở ngoại vi vương quốc của vua, trong khi

84. Tarthang Tulku (1994), Holy Places of the Buddha, Crytal Mirror, Volume Nine, Dharma Press, USA.

85. Balkrishna Govind Gokhale, *Ashoka Maurya* (USA: Irvington. Publishers, 1966), 223, 228, 231

những cây cột được dựng dọc theo những con đường chính, là nơi những người hành hương tụ tập. Các sắc lệnh được viết bằng chính lời của Đại đế A-dục. Các sắc lệnh ấy đã được tìm thấy ở hơn ba mươi địa điểm trên khắp Ấn Độ, Nepal, Pakistan và Afghanistan. Hầu hết chúng được viết bằng ngôn ngữ của các nơi này.

Đại đế A-dục đã tham gia vào việc truyền bá Phật giáo thông qua các sắc lệnh bằng các khối đá, khắc lên vách đá, nhiều trụ cột được dựng lên trong đế chế của vua và hơn thế nữa. Dòng chữ Bhabru kêu gọi người dân tôn trọng, có niềm tin vào Phật, Pháp và Tăng. Đạo đức cá nhân mà Đại đế A-dục hy vọng sẽ thúc đẩy bao gồm sự kính trọng đối với cha mẹ, người lớn tuổi, thầy cô, bạn bè, người hầu, người khổ hạnh và Bà la môn. Các sắc lệnh nằm trên đá Girnar cũng nhấn mạnh "ba bổn phận hiếu thảo của người con".

Đại đế A-dục cũng khuyến khích sự cúng dường (dana), không sát hại đối với cuộc sống (avihimsa bhutanam), điều độ trong chi tiêu, tiết kiệm, đàng hoàng, học hỏi và đối xử tốt với các tôn giáo khác. Những phẩm chất của trái tim được Đại đế A-dục khuyến nghị trong các sắc lệnh cho thấy tâm linh sâu sắc của vua. Chúng bao gồm lòng tốt, sự tự kiểm điểm, sự trung thực, lòng biết ơn, sự trong sáng của trái tim, sự nhiệt tình, lòng trung thành, sự tự chủ và tình đạo đối với giáo Pháp như sau:

"*Theo bảy bản kinh Phật giáo sau đây được khuyến khích cho cả Tăng đoàn và cư sĩ. Những bản kinh được vua A-dục yêu thích này dường như mô tả cuộc sống thiền môn của các nhà sư, và các tiêu chuẩn đạo đức mà vua đã cống hiến. Vua ít để ý đến triết lý nhiều mà quan tâm đến ứng dụng đạo đức và thực tiễn của Phật pháp. Munigatha* được ca ngợi là vị ẩn sĩ nỗ lực tự tu tập chính mình để tìm sự tĩnh lặng đoạn trừ tất cả lậu hoặc, có trí tuệ, giới hạnh và định lực. Kinh Mauneya ca ngợi sự bình lặng và thanh tịnh của đời sống ẩn dật. Kinh Rahulovada, Đức Phật khuyên Rahula chống lại lời nói dối một cách có ý thức. Upatissapasine là nơi Ngài Xá lợi phất (Sariputta) thường quán chiếu nội tĩnh."[86]

3.6. Truyền thuyết về Đại Đế A-dục (Ashoka-vadana)

Trụ cột Đại đế A-dục ở Vườn Lâm-tì-ni (Lumbini), nơi sinh của Đức Phật, Nepal

Ashoka-vadana là một văn bản thế kỷ thứ hai liên quan đến truyền thuyết về Đại đế A-dục. tác phẩm đã được Đại sư Pháp Hiền vào năm 300 dịch sang tiếng Trung Quốc. Đây thực chất là một bản văn nguyên thủy, và ngôn ngữ thuộc dân tộc Mathura Tây bắc Ấn Độ. Trọng tâm của văn bản ít được biết đến này là khám phá mối quan hệ giữa nhà vua A-Dục với Tăng đoàn (cộng đồng các nhà sư) và thiết lập một đời sống thiền môn lý tưởng cho Phật tử và dân chúng bằng cách kể những câu chuyện đạo vị về sự

86. http://www.suttas.com/king-Aśoka.html

vi diệu của Phật giáo. Đại đế A-dục đã sử dụng quyền lực nhà nước để truyền bá Phật giáo một cách mạnh mẽ và hiệu quả.

3.7. Phúc lợi cho loài động vật

Các sắc lệnh bằng đá của Đại đế A-dục tuyên bố rằng việc làm tổn thương các sinh vật sống là không tốt và không nên để một con vật nào bị hy sinh để làm thịt. Tuy nhiên, vua không cấm giết mổ gia súc thông thường hoặc ăn thịt bò.

Triều đại của Đại đế A-dục Maurya có thể đã biến mất vào lịch sử khi thời gian trôi qua, nếu vua không để lại những ghi chép về triều đại của Ngài. Những ghi chép này khắc ở các cột đá điêu khắc nói về những hành động, lời khuyến nhủ, cảnh cáo hay sắc lịnh nghiêm khắc được đóng dấu với tên của Đại đế A-dục. Các ngôn ngữ được sử dụng là một trong những ngôn ngữ phổ biến của Prakrit được khắc bằng chữ trong văn bản Brahmi.

"*Vua Ashoka, vị vua thứ ba của triều đại Mauryan Ấn Độ, cũng được coi là "một trong những nhà cai trị mẫu mực nhất từng được biết đến.*"[87]

3.8. Vương quyền Phật giáo (Pháp trị)

Một trong những di sản lâu dài hơn của Đại đế A-dục Maurya là mô hình mà vua đã đưa ra cho mối quan hệ giữa Phật giáo và nhà nước cai trị (dùng pháp trị dân). Mô hình quyền cai trị do Đại đế A-dục thể hiện đã thay thế quan niệm về vương quyền thần thánh trước đây thống trị (ví dụ như ở vương quốc Angkor). Dưới mô hình "vương quyền Phật giáo" này, nhà vua đã tìm cách hợp pháp hóa sự cai trị của mình không phải thông qua nguồn gốc thần thánh,

---

87. N.A. Nikam and Richard McKeon, The Edicts of Ashoka (Chicago: Chicago University Press, 1959), 47, 52.

mà bằng cách hỗ trợ và được sự chấp thuận của Tăng đoàn Phật giáo.

Theo gương của Đại đế A-dục, các vị vua đã thành lập các tu viện, tài trợ cho việc xây dựng các bảo tháp, và ủng hộ việc xuất gia của các nhà sư trong vương quốc của họ. Nhiều nhà cai trị cũng đã đóng một vai trò tích cực trong giải quyết các tranh chấp về địa vị và quy định của Tăng đoàn, như Đại đế A-dục đã làm khi triệu tập một cuộc họp kín để giải quyết một số vấn đề gây tranh cãi trong Tăng đoàn dưới triều đại của vua. Sự phát triển này cuối cùng đã dẫn đến một sự liên kết chặt chẽ ở nhiều nước Đông Nam Á giữa chế độ quân chủ và Phật giáo hệ thống phân cấp, một hiệp hội mà ngày nay vẫn có thể được nhìn thấy trong Phật giáo được nhà nước hỗ trợ của Thái Lan và vai trò truyền thống của nhà vua Thái Lan với tư cách là một nhà lãnh đạo tôn giáo và đất nước. Đại đế A-dục cũng nói rằng tất cả các cận thần của vua luôn cai trị người dân một cách có đạo đức.

3.9. Nguồn Khảo Cổ Học Lịch Sử của Đại đế A-dục

Nhà khảo cổ học James Prinsep đã đóng góp trong sự liên hệ về nguồn lịch sử Đại đế A-dục. Một nhà sử học quan trọng khác nữa là nhà khảo cổ học người Anh John Hubert Marshall, Tổng Giám đốc Khảo sát Khảo cổ Ấn Độ. Niềm hứng thú của ông Marshall là khám phá tháp Sanchi và Sarnath, thêm đó là Harappa và Mohenjodaro đều có liên quan đến Đại đế A-dục. Ngài Alexander Cunningham, một nhà khảo cổ học và là kỹ sư quân đội người Anh, thường được biết đến là cha đẻ Khảo cổ của Ấn Độ, công bố các di sản có công của Đại đế A-dục như Bảo tháp Bharhut, Sarnath, Sanchi, và chùa Mahabodhi. Mortimer Wheeler, một nhà khảo cổ học người Anh, cũng đã tiếp xúc với nguồn lịch sử "*Ashokan*", đặc biệt là Taxila. Chữ khắc song ngữ (tiếng Hy Lạp và tiếng Aramaic) của Đại đế A-dục được phát hiện tại Kandahar (Bảo tàng Quốc gia

Afghanistan).

Chữ khắc trong các sắc lệnh của Đại đế A-dục

Một bản khắc của Đại đế A-dục nói về Giới Sát Sanh như sau: "Đại đế A-dục ra lệnh cấm giết tất cả các sinh vật bốn chân dù có lợi ích hay không, và không được ăn chúng. Hơn nữa, một số loài động vật cụ thể bao gồm một số loài chim, một số loại cá và bò đực không nên hại chúng. Vua cũng cấm giết dê cái, cừu và lợn đang cho con bú nuôi chúng cho đến ít nhất sáu tháng tuổi. Vua cũng "cấm giết tất cả cá và thiến động vật trong những thời kỳ *nhất định như* vào ngày Chaturmasa và Uposatha."[88]

Đại đế A-dục cũng bãi bỏ việc săn bắn động vật và hạn chế giết động vật để làm thức ăn trong hoàng gia. Bởi vì chính Đại đế A-dục đã bỏ thú vui săn bắn, không ăn thịt vào nhiều ngày lễ, cũng như thành lập nhiều phòng

88. Dharmapal, *Ashoka–2300,* 70, 72.

khám thú y. Đế chế Mauryan dưới thời Đại đế A-dục đã được mô tả là một trong rất ít trường hợp trong lịch sử thế giới của một chính phủ đối xử với động vật của mình như những người công dân và xứng đáng được bảo vệ với tư cách là cư dân của con người, nhân quyền và súc quyền.

3.10. Các Trụ đá của Đại đế A-dục (Aśokastambha)

Các trụ cột của Đại đế A-dục là một loạt các cột được dựng khắp miền bắc Ấn Độ tiểu lục địa và được xây dựng bởi Vua A-dục vào thế kỷ thứ ba trước Công nguyên. Ban đầu, chắc hẳn đã có nhiều trụ cột của Đại đế A-dục mặc dù chỉ có mười trụ cột có chữ khắc vẫn còn bảo tồn. Tính chiều cao trung bình từ 40 đến 50 feet và nặng tới 50 tấn mỗi cột. Tất cả các cột đều được khai thác tại Chunar, ngay phía nam Varanasi, và kéo khiêng đôi khi hàng trăm dặm, tới nơi chúng đã được dựng lên ngày nay.

3.11. Trụ đá Sư tử của Đại đế A-dục (Sarnath, Varanasi)

Tại Vườn Lộc Uyển (Sanarth), một thành phố ở bang Uttar Pradesh, Đông Ấn Độ, cách Varanasi 13km về phía Đông bắc, gần ngã ba sông Hằng và sông Gormati. Đây là nơi Đức Thế Tôn lăn chuyển bánh xe Chánh Pháp đầu tiên, vua A Dục cũng đã đến chiêm bái, cho dựng một trụ đá rất lớn (đường kính 7 tấc, cao 15,25 mét) để đánh dấu nơi Đức Thế Tôn thiết lập Tam Bảo, mở đầu công cuộc truyền bá Chánh Pháp. Chính đá sư tử nơi này đã trở thành quốc huy của Ấn Độ ngày nay.

Thomas Cory đã tìm thấy trụ cột đầu tiên của Vua Adục vào thế kỷ 16 trong đống đổ nát. Trụ có khắc bánh xe pháp đại diện cho mặt trời hay giáo pháp. Chữ "Vạn" (swastika) tượng trưng cho vũ trụ đang nhảy xung quanh trục trung tâm, có các vị thần bảo vệ chống lại cái ác. Cột trụ sư tử của Đại đế A-dục là một điêu khắc bốn con sư tử đứng quay lưng lại với nhau. Ban đầu nó được đặt trên đỉnh Trụ cột Vua A-dục tại Sarnath, nay thuộc bang Uttar Pradesh, Ấn Độ. Cột đá này, đôi khi được gọi là Cột Ashoka, vẫn ở vị trí ban đầu tức khu khảo cổ Sarnath, trong khi đỉnh cột bốn con sư tử hiện được trưng bày tại Viện Bảo tàng Khảo Cổ Sarnath, Varanasi, đối diện với Khu thánh Tích Sarnath.

Quốc huy và Quốc kỳ Ấn Độ với hình trụ đá bốn Sư tử của Đại đế A-dục

Trụ đá Sư tử của Đại đế A-dục này đã được chọn làm Quốc huy của Ấn Độ. Thì "bánh xe Luân xa Ashoka" được đặt tại trung tâm của lá Quốc kỳ (ba màu, bánh xe chuyển pháp luân nằm giữa màu trắng của quốc kỳ). Trụ đá có bốn con sư tử (Sư tử Ấn Độ/Châu Á) quay lưng vào nhau trên đỉnh cột, với một đường viền tròn khắc hình con voi, ngựa, bò đực và sư tử, xen kẽ là bánh xe pháp, hoa sen hình chuông. Trụ đá nguyên khối bóng lưỡng tuyệt đẹp. Chúng được khắc từ một khối đá sa thạch bóng loáng duy nhất. Trụ đá được tôn vinh là "Bánh xe Pháp" (Pháp luân, Dharmachakra, thường được biết đến ở Ấn Độ là Luân xa Ashoka).

Trụ đá sư tử Ashoka hay trụ đá sư tử Sarnath còn được biết đến là biểu tượng quốc gia của Ấn Độ. Trụ đá Sarnath mang một trong những Sắc lệnh của Đại đế A-dục. Một dòng chữ ghi trên bia với ý đồ kêu gọi đoàn kết trong nội bộ Tăng đoàn, trong đó viết như sau, ***"Không ai được gây chia rẽ trong hàng tu sĩ".*** Cột Sarnath là một cột có đầu trụ bao quanh, bao gồm một mái che tượng trưng cho một hoa sen hình chuông ngược, đỉnh cột hình trụ ngắn có bốn bánh xe Pháp luân với hai mươi bốn căm xe, bốn con vật (voi, bò tót, ngựa và sư tử). Bốn con vật ở Sarnath vốn được cho là tượng trưng cho các giai đoạn khác nhau trong cuộc đời của Đức Phật.

Trụ đá Sư tử Ashoka được trưng bày tại Viện Bảo tàng Khảo cổ học Sarnath, Varanasi. Đây là hồn thiêng quốc huy của Ấn Độ; biểu tượng quốc gia đã được sử dụng trong hầu hết các tài liệu của chính phủ từ thời cổ đại đến nay.

Con voi tượng trưng cho tư tưởng của Đức Phật liên quan đến giấc mơ của Hoàng hậu Maya về voi trắng sáu ngà chui vào bụng mẫu hậu Maya.

. Con Bò tượng trưng cho dục vọng trần thế khi còn là một thái tử đã trải nghiệm qua.

. Con ngựa tượng trưng cho Thái tử từ giả cuộc sống vương giả.

. Con Sư Tử tượng trưng cho sự thành tựu Phật quả.

Bên cạnh những cách giải thích mang tính Phật giáo như trên, còn có một số cách giải thích khác về biểu tượng của trụ cột Đại đế A-dục tại Sarnath như *"Bốn con sư tử tượng trưng cho sự cai trị của Đại đế A-dục ở khắp bốn phương; các bánh xe là biểu tượng của sự cai trị giác ngộ của Ngài (Chakravartin) và bốn động vật là biểu tượng của bốn vùng lãnh thổ liền kề của Ấn Độ."*[89]

Sau đây là một số pháp trị thấm nhuần đạo lý nhằm mục đích tạo một xã hội bất bạo động và hòa bình như sau:

1. *Samyam hay làm chủ giác quan.*
2. *Bhavasuddhi hay tư tưởng trong sạch.*
3. *Kritajnata hay lòng biết ơn.*
4. *Dridh-bhakti hay lòng tin bất động.*
5. *Daya hay lòng tốt.*
6. *Dana hay từ thiện.*
7. *Saucha hay sự thuần khiết, trong sáng.*
8. *Satya hay sự trung thực.*
9. *Sushrust hoặc là sự phục vụ.*
10. *Sampritipatti hoặc là sự hỗ trợ.*
11. *Apichiti hoặc là sự hỗ trợ (Sắc lệnh trên đá Kalinga xii và xiii)*[90]

"Trụ cột Vua A-dục: một loạt các cột được dựng khắp

---

89. Giand Chand Chauhan, *Origin and Growth of Feudalism in Early India: From the Mauryas to AD 650.* (Delhi: Munshiram Manoharlal Publishers, 2004), 186, 192; V.D. Mahajan, *Kalinga Rock Edicts–Ancient India*, (New Delhi: S. Chand and Co. Ltd. Publishers, 2008), 300, 304.

90. D.B. Kiskalar, "Literary Value of Inscriptions of Ashoka," *Journal of Indian History* (New Delhi), 226

tiểu lục địa Ấn Độ và mang những dòng chữ gửi đến các chư Tôn thiền đức Tăng Ni.Trong số tất cả những cột đá do Đại đế A-dục dựng lên, chỉ có 20 cây còn được bảo tồn nguyên vẹn. Trong số hai mươi tác phẩm này, chỉ có bảy tác phẩm điêu khắc các loài động vật được bảo quản tốt cho đến ngày nay."[91]

Các nhà khảo cổ khai quật tìm thấy rất nhiều nền tháp (thờ xá lợi Phật), chùa, tu viện, cột đá, bia ký rải rác trên khắp Ấn Độ cũng như ở các quốc gia Nepal, Pakistan và Afghanistan. Những trụ đá này được điêu khắc một cách tinh xảo đầy mỹ thuật . Đây là một đóng góp sớm nhất của nền văn minh thung lũng Ấn Hà, một loại cổ ngữ của Harrapa, xưa hơn cả cỗ ngữ Sanskrit, loại ngôn ngữ thường thấy ở các trụ đá mà ngày nay gọi là Prakrita. Các chữ khắc cho thấy sự nỗ lực của Đại đế A-dục đã kiến thiết chính sách an dân theo pháp lục hòa, một quốc gia dựa trên nền tảng đạo đức Phật Giáo, giữ giới luật tránh ác làm lành, như một cột trụ ghi: *"Nếu quần chúng sau khi nghe được lời Phật dạy, thực hành, sẽ đạt được lợi ích trong Chánh Pháp.*"[92]

Vua khuyên người dân thực hành "*không sát sanh, hiếu kính cha mẹ và các bậc trưởng thượng, tôn trọng thầy cô giáo, cung kính cúng dường các Sa Môn, Bà La Môn, xử sự tốt với thân bằng quyến thuộc, chia sẻ với bạn bè, đối đãi nhân hậu với kẻ làm công, người giúp việc, giúp đỡ người già, người nghèo khó, kẻ khổ đau.*"[93] Ngoài ra trong một bia ký khác, vua A Dục đã cho khắc bản Kinh

---

91. https://fairgaze.com/fgnews/the-pillars-of-ashoka_92319.html

92. John S. Strong: The Legend of King Ashoka (Princeton University Press), 1983.

93. Lược theo bản Việt dịch của HT Thích Thiện Châu. Đại đế A-dục, Một ông vua hộ trì phật pháp. Thích Nguyên Tạng. 09/09/2015. https://thuvienhoasen.org/a23735/dai-de-a-duc-mot-ong-vua-ho-tri-phat-phap

Chân Hạnh Phúc (Mahamangala Sutta)[94] như sau:

Chư thiên và loài người
Suy nghĩ về hạnh phúc
Ước mong được hạnh phúc
Chân hạnh phúc là gì?

Thế Tôn đáp kệ rằng:
Kẻ si mê nên tránh
Bậc hiền đức phải gần
Cung kính người đáng kính
Ấy là chân hạnh phúc.

Chọn nơi lành mà ở
Đời trước đã tạo phúc
Nay giữ lòng thẳng ngay
Ấy là chân hạnh phúc.

Hiểu rộng và khéo tay
Giữ tròn các giới luật
Nói những lời hòa ái
Ấy là chân hạnh phúc.

Cung dưỡng cha mẹ già
Yêu mến vợ /chồng và con
Không vương vấn phiền hà

94. Kinh Chân Hạnh Phúc (Maha Mangala Sutta). Việt dịch: Hoà Thượng Thiện Châu.
https://binhnhon.wordpress.com/

Ấy là chân hạnh phúc.

Cho và sống đúng cách
Nên giúp đỡ bà con
Hành động không chê trách
Ấy là chân hạnh phúc.

Ngăn trừ điều ác xấu
Dứt bỏ thói rượu chè
Chuyên cần trong Chánh Đạo
Ấy là chân hạnh phúc.

Kính nhường và khiêm tốn
Biết đủ và nhớ ơn
Tuỳ thời học đạo lý
Ấy là chân hạnh phúc.

Nhẫn nhục vâng ý lành
Viếng thăm bậc tu hành
Tuỳ thời bàn luận đạo
Ấy là chân hạnh phúc.

Trong sạch và siêng năng
Suốt thông các chân lý
Thực hiện vui Niết Bàn
Ấy là chân hạnh phúc.

Tiếp xúc với thế gian

Giữ lòng không sa ngã
Không sầu nhiễm bình an
Ấy là chân hạnh phúc.
Như thế mà tu hành
Việc gì cũng thành tựu
Ở đâu cũng an lành
Ấy là chân hạnh phúc."

Ashoka Pillar in Lumbini (the birthplace of Buddha), Nepal

Ý nghĩa bài kinh rất rõ ràng cụ thể, được dân chúng thấu hiểu thực hiện vào cuộc sống hằng ngày do đó xã hội thời vua A Dục sau khi vua giác ngộ rất an bình hạnh phúc (nghĩa là nên tránh người si mê, gần bậc hiền đức; Chọn nơi lành mà ở, luôn giữ lòng thẳng ngay; Hiểu rộng và khéo tay, giữ tròn các giới luật, nói lời hòa ái; Cung dưỡng cha mẹ già, yêu mến vợ /chồng và con, không vương vấn phiền hà; Bố thí, giúp đỡ bà con, hành động không chê trách; Ngăn trừ điều ác xấu, dứt bỏ thói rượu chè, siêng năng trong Chánh Đạo; Kính nhường và khiêm tốn, biết đủ và nhớ ơn, tùy thời học đạo lý; Nhẫn nhục vâng ý lành, viếng thăm bậc tu hành, tùy thời bàn luận đạo; Trong sạch và siêng năng, suốt thông các chân lý, thực hiện vui Niết Bàn; Tiếp xúc với thế gian, giữ lòng không sa ngã, không sầu nhiễm bình an).

Tại thánh tích Lâm Tỳ Ni (Lumbini), Nepal, nơi Đức Phật đản sanh. Đại đế A-dục đã cho dựng một trụ đá cao 15 mét, hiện nay vẫn còn tại thánh tích này, có thể nói đây là trụ đá còn nguyên vẹn, được bao bọc bởi một hàng rào sắt để bảo hộ. Trên trụ đá này vẫn còn thấy hàng chữ như sau: *"Sau hai mươi năm lên ngôi, vua Priyadarsi (Vương hiệu của Vua A Dục), người được chư thiên yêu mến, đã thân hành viếng thăm và lễ bái nơi đây, bởi vì chính tại nơi này Đức Phật Thích Ca đã được ra đời."*[95]

Tại thành Tỳ Xá Ly (Vaishali, Vesāli), một thành phố cổ đại, ngày nay thuộc huyện Vaishali bang Bihar, Đông Ấn Độ. Đây là nơi Đức Phật hay dừng chân để giảng pháp, an cư mùa mưa, cho phép Di mẫu Kiều-đàm-di Đại Ái Đạo (Mahā Pajāpatī Gotamī, Ma-ha ba-xà ba-đề) cùng hàng nữ giới xuất gia, là quê hương của bồ tát tại gia cư sĩ Duy-ma-cật, nơi Tôn Giả A-nan nhập niết bàn. Vua A-dục xây một tu viện ở đây cho Tăng đoàn cũng như có dựng một trụ đá để tưởng nhớ Đức Phật và các thánh tổ tại nơi này.

Tại thị trấn Sanchi thuộc quận Raisen của bang Madhya Pradesh, Ấn Độ, một thành phố miền Trung Ấn Độ, cách Bom Bay khoảng 549 dặm, Vua A Dục đã cho xây dựng một tu viện và một Đại Bảo Tháp tại nơi này với những nét điêu khắc và hoa văn rất tinh tế tuyệt mỹ.

95. Lumbini Development Trust, Genesis Publishing, Kathmandu, Nepal/1988

Sư cô TN Giới Hương quỳ trước khu Thánh Tích Xá-vệ, Ấn Độ, với Cột đá Vua A Dục còn nguyên vẹn trang nghiêm, tháng 9 năm 2003

3.12. Vua A Dục tổ chức kết tập kinh điển lần thứ ba

Khoảng năm 308 trước Công nguyên, trong thời trị vì của Đại đế A Dục, Đại hội Kết tập kinh điển lần thứ ba được tổ chức tại Tự viện Asokamara, thành phố Hoa Thị Thành (Pataliputta) để thảo luận về những điểm dị biệt trong luận thuyết của các Tỳ kheo (Bhikshu) thuộc các bộ phái khác nhau.

Tương truyền, Tăng đoàn lúc đó đã bị một số người trà

trộn và lạm dụng, gây nhiều bất hòa nội bộ. Do vậy, Đại hội Kết tập kinh điển lần thứ ba với sự tham dự của 1000 vị Tỳ kheo tinh thông tam tạng, với mục đích thanh lọc những vị tăng dị giáo, bác bỏ những quan điểm dị giáo của ngoại đạo, bảo tồn sự thanh tịnh của Phật Pháp.

Người chủ trì Đại hội Kết tập kinh điển, Ngài Mục Kiền Liên Tử Đế Tu (Moggaliputta Tissa), đã soạn một luận thư *"Thuyết sự"* (Luận Tạng KathàvatT.N.u) để phản bác nghĩa lý của các phái ngoại đạo đương thời.

Lần kết tập kỳ thứ ba này kéo dài trong chín tháng, kết quả là Phật pháp trở lại thanh tịnh và ổn định.

3.13. Đại đế A-dục có công truyền bá Phật pháp qua Caylon (Sri Lanka)

Theo sau cuộc Kết Tập Kinh Điển lần thứ 3 (năm 254 trước Công Nguyên), Vua A Dục đã cử nhiều phái đoàn hoằng pháp ra nước ngoài như Tích Lan, Miến Điện, Mã Lai và Sumatra.

Vua A-dục đã cử hai người con là hoàng thái tử Mahinda và công chúa Singhamiha xuất gia làm Tăng Ni, gia nhập Tăng đoàn tu học và sau đó được gởi sang Tích Lan để hoằng pháp. Điều này được nói trong cuốn Ashokavadana tiếng Phạn (Truyền Thuyết về Ashoka), được viết vào thế kỷ thứ hai, và biên niên sử tiếng Pāli của Sri Lanka (Dipavamsa và Mahavamsa), vv…

3.13.1. Thánh tăng Mahā Mahinda Thero (Con trai của Vua A-dục) truyền pháp đầu tiên tại Ceylon

Cuộc kiết tập Phật giáo lần thứ ba (khoảng năm 250 trước Công nguyên) tại thành phố Pataliputta, Ấn Độ, là một giai đoạn quan trọng trong lịch sử Phật giáo bởi vì đó là thời điểm Phật giáo Nguyên Thủy (Theravāda) được truyền vào Sri Lanka. Và chính nhờ công đức của Vua

A-dục đã cử con trai là Thánh tăng Mahā Mahinda Thero và con gái là Tỳ Kheo Ni Sanghamittā Theri đến Celon (Sri Lanka cổ đại) để truyền bá Phật pháp.

Photo: Tranh Thánh tăng Mahinda mang Phật giáo vào Sri Lanka. Họa sĩ D. G. Somapala[96]

Lịch sử Phật Giáo của Sri Lanka được khởi đầu từ ngày Tỳ kheo Thera Mahinda (Sinhala: මිහිඳු මහරහතන් වහන්සේ), con trai của Đại Đế A Dục (Aśoka hoặc Dhammaśoka) từ Ấn độ đến Sri Lanka hoằng pháp vào triều đại Vua Devānampiya Tissa (236 năm sau hoàng đế Vijaya). Ngài thuyết giảng giáo pháp cho dân chúng nghe, họ có thể lãnh hội tiếp nhận bức thông điệp giải thoát của Đức Bổn Sư Thích Ca và nhanh chóng ứng dụng trong đời sống hàng ngày của mình. Từ đó, Phật pháp diệu huyền được lan truyền khắp hải đảo. Điều này cho thấy năng lượng từ bi, truyền đạo và giác ngộ của bậc thánh tăng A La Hán Thera Mahinda như lời di giáo của Đức Từ Phụ Thế Tôn: "Các thầy Tỳ-kheo hãy đến các vùng mà các

96. https://www.sundaytimes.lk/180624/funday-times/arahant-mahinda-brings-buddhism-to-sri-lanka-299140.html

thầy thích, đừng để hai người cùng đi một chỗ. Dạy và giảng pháp cho nhiều người trong khả năng của mình," hay "Khi xuất hiện ở đời, đem lại hạnh phúc và an lạc cho số đông, vì lợi ích, vì hạnh phúc, vì an lạc cho chư Thiên và loài người."[97]

Sáu mươi tám hang động tu tập do Thánh Tăng Mahinda hướng dẫn. Hình chụp ngày 11/7/2023

97. Tăng Chi Bộ I, chương 1, phẩm Một người, phần Như Lai [lược], VNCPHVN ấn hành, 1996, tr 46.

Theo biên niên sử, hoàng đế A Dục và Vua Devānampiya Tissa (Sri Lanka) là hai người bạn hàng xóm láng giềng giao hảo rất thân, dù chưa có duyên diện kiến nhau. Vua Devānampiya Tissa thường gởi đại thần quan trọng hay những nhà sứ giả đem vật phẩm quý giá tặng nước Ấn Độ đáp tình lại, Vua A Dục cũng thường gởi phái đoàn truyền giáo ngoại giao đến Sri Lanka, như gởi con trai là tỳ kheo Thera Mahinda đến Sri Lanka để giới thiệu Phật giáo với bức thông điệp đầy pháp vị như sau:

"Tôi đã quy y với Phật bảo (Đức Thế Tôn), với Pháp Bảo (giáo pháp của Ngài), và với Tăng Bảo (chư tăng trong Giáo Hội). Chính tôi đã tuyên bố rằng mình là một thiện tín cư sĩ trong tôn giáo của Đức Thích Ca. Giờ đây thưa Đại Vương, ôi! Ngài là bậc quý nhất trong dân chúng, đã dùng Phật pháp để chuyển hóa tâm mình, hãy quy y với Tam Bảo (ba ngôi quý giá nhất) trong các bảo vật."

(Aha.m Buddhañ ca Dhammañ ca Sanghañ ca sara. na.mgato upaasakatta.m vedesi.m Saakyaputtassa saasane tvamp'imaani ratanaani uttamaani naruttama citta.m pasaadayitvaana saddhaaya sara.na.m bhaja.)

(I have taken refuge in the Buddha, his Doctrine and his Order, I have declared myself a lay-disciple in the religion of the Saakya son; seek then, O best of men, refuge in these best of gems, converting your mind with believing heart.)[98]

Vào ngày trăng tròn tháng Jetta, Phật Lịch năm 236 (tức 308 trước Công nguyên, nhằm năm thứ mười tám triều đại Vua A Dục), thánh tăng Mahā Mahinda cùng với đoàn truyền giáo Ấn Độ đến đỉnh núi Missaka, một ngọn núi cao nổi bật giữa những cánh đồng phì nhiêu xung quanh thuộc thị trấn Mihintale hiện nay (cách phía Đông thủ đô Anurādhapura 8 dặm Anh). Vua Devānampiya Tissa đã cung kính đón rước đoàn truyền giáo của Thánh

98. Buddhism in Sri Lanka: A Short History, by H.R. Perera, 2007. https://www.accesstoinsight.org/lib/authors/perera/wheel100.html#sect-47

tăng Mahā Mahinda tại thủ đô Anurādhapura. Kinh Cūla Hatthi-padopama Sutta (Majjhima Nikāya, Trung Bộ Kinh, 27) là bài pháp mà Ngài Mahā Mahinda thuyết giảng cho vua nói về ý nghĩa quy y Tam Bảo (Phật Bảo, Pháp Bảo và Tăng Bảo), đời sống xuất gia của chư tăng, và trí minh sát tuệ. Sau đó, vua cùng nhiều quan chức và dân chúng thọ tam quy ngũ giới làm đệ tử Phật.[99]

Photo trái sang: Sư cô Viên Nhuận, Sư Siri Sumedha, Ns T.N. Giới Hương, Sư cô Viên Bảo và Ni cô Viên Lành, chụp đường lên Đỉnh Đại tháp Mihintale ngày 11/7/2023

99. Phật giáo tại Sri Lanka, Piyadassi Manhāthera, Phạm Kim Khánh dịch.https://www.vomonthientu.org/a356/14-phat-giao-tai-sri-lanka-

Nhà vua có tâm đạo thuần thành, sắp xếp cho các thiện tín xa gần đến nghe giáo pháp của Đức Thế Tôn. Bài thuyết giảng của Đức thánh tăng Mahā Mahinda có sức cảm hóa mạnh mẽ khiến ai cũng lãnh hội những lời dạy từ bi và trí tuệ của Đức Phật. Không bao lâu, bức thông điệp của Đức Bổn Sư nhanh chóng vang khắp các vùng của hải đảo. Phật giáo chánh thức được công nhận và giáo hội tăng già của các tỳ kheo (Bhikkhu Sangha) cũng được thành lập. Đây là dấu mốc lịch sử cho thấy bộ phái Phật giáo Nguyên Thuỷ được truyền ra khỏi Ấn Độ, lưu truyền đến Sri Lanka dưới triều đại vua Devànampiyatissa. Sri Lanka trở thành một trung tâm của Phật giáo trên thế giới từ thời cổ đại.

3.13.2. Thánh tổ Tỳ Kheo Ni Sanghamittā Theri (con gái của Vua A-dục) thành lập Giáo Hội Ni ở Ceylon

Hoàng Hậu Anulā, thứ phi của một vị phó vương tên Mahānāga, cùng với 500 thị nữ đến nghe pháp, tha thiết xin thánh tăng Mahinda cho xuất gia theo dấu chân của Đức Thế Tôn. Tuy nhiên, vào lúc bấy giờ ở Sri Lanka chưa có Giáo Hội Tỳ Kheo Ni và theo giới luật, Ngài Mahinda không có quyền chủ trì lễ xuất gia cho người nữ, chỉ có một vị Phật hay Giáo Hội Tỳ Kheo Ni mới có quyền. Do đó, Đức Mahinda gợi ý Vua Devānampiya Tissa cung thỉnh Vua A-dục cho phép con gái là Tỳ-kheo-ni Sanghamittā, em gái của Ngài, lúc ấy là một Tỳ kheo ni tại Ấn độ, qua Sri Lanka làm lễ xuất gia cho hàng phụ nữ và thành lập Giáo Hội Tỳ Kheo Ni (Bhikkhunī Sangha).

Vua Devānampiya Tissa lấy làm hoan hỷ cung thỉnh, Vua A Dục chấp thuận cho công chúa tức Tỳ-kheo-ni Sanghamittā Theri đến Sri Lanka truyền giáo Ni. Thánh Tổ đã mang theo một nhánh cây bồ đề được chiết từ cây Bồ đề bên sông Ni-Liên,[100] nơi Đức Thế Tôn đã ngồi thiền

100. Sông Ni Liên Thiền (Naranjana) cách tháp Đại Tháp khoảng 200 mét về phía Đông. Ngày nay sông này có tên là Lilajan, sông rộng trên 1

49 ngày và giác ngộ.

Ni sư Giới Hương chụp với Chư Ni trước tượng Thánh tổ Sanghamittā Their tại chùa Susilavasa ngày 19/7/2023

Vua Devānampiya Tissa tổ chức một buổi lễ vô cùng long trọng để nhận cây Bồ Đề thiêng và trồng tại khu vườn Megha Garden, thủ đô Anurādhapura. Hiện nay, cây vẫn tươi tốt sum suê dù trải qua hơn 2600 năm, hàng triệu khách trên thế giới đến đây để hành hương chiêm bái thường xuyên. Cây cổ thụ bồ đề được ghi nhận là cây lớn tuổi nhất trên thế giới,[101] 2272 năm tuổi (2023+249 = 2270 năm). Từ cội gốc này, nhiều nhánh cây con đã được chiết và trồng ở nhiều tu viện trên đảo Sri Lanka và nhiều chùa trên thế giới.

Riêng trưởng lão Tỳ-kheo-ni Sanghamittā Theri được

---

cây số, vào mùa nắng sông khô cạn không còn một giọt nước, nhưng đến mùa mưa thì nước chảy rất mạnh. Theo truyền thống Phật Giáo thì chính tại nơi này Đức Phật đã tắm gội sạch sẽ, sau đó Ngài nhận bát cháo sữa do nàng Sujata cúng dường, rồi Ngài nhận thêm bó cỏ kiết tường làm gối ngồi thiền từ một nông dân trong vùng, trước khi Ngài đi về cội Bồ Đề bắt đầu thiền định.
https://chuaphuoclinh.net/goc-lich-su-song-ni-lien-thien-.html

101. Sri Maha Bodhi – The Sacred Bo Tree http://amazinglanka.com/wp/sri-maha-bodhi-the-sacred-bo-tree/

xem là Thánh Tổ Ni giới ở Phật giáo Sri Lanka vì nhờ Ngài truyền giới mà từ đó Ni đoàn được thành lập, tồn tại và phát triển đến ngày nay. Nên hầu như chùa Ni Sri Lanka nào cũng thờ tượng của thánh tổ Saṅghamittā Theri.

Vì vậy, hoàng đế A-dục có công đức rất lớn vì đã gửi con trai của mình, thái tử tức Tỳ kheo Mahinda (Mahendra), đến Tích Lan để thành lập Phật giáo tại hải đảo Ceylon, sau đó, đã gửi con gái của mình, Công chúa Sanghamitra, sang Tích Lan để thực hành lễ xuất gia cho chư Ni, thành lập Ni đoàn, truyền bá con đường chân lý giải thoát. Từ đó, Phật giáo, đặc biệt Nam truyền (Theravada), đã phát triển thành quốc giáo tại hải đảo Sri Lanka này.

3.14. Đại đế A-dục thăng hà và di sản để lại

Bản đá sắc lệnh của Đại đế A-dục tại Junagadh có khắc những dòng chữ của Vua (mười bốn bản sắc lệnh của Ashoka), Rudradaman I, và Skandagupta. Đại đế A-dục cai trị trong khoảng ba mươi sáu năm. Truyền thuyết theo những dòng khắc ghi rằng trong quá trình hỏa táng, cơ thể của Đại đế A-dục đã cháy trong bảy ngày đêm. Sau khi Đại đế A-dục qua đời, các Triều đại Mauryan chỉ tồn tại thêm năm mươi năm nữa cho đến khi đế chế của Đại đế A-dục trải rộng trên hầu hết tiểu lục địa Ấn Độ.

Đại đế A-dục có nhiều vợ và con, nhưng nhiều tên của họ đã bị thất lạc theo thời gian. Phối ngẫu chính (agramahisi) là Asandhimitra, người dường như không sinh con cho Vua. Ở tuổi già, dường như Đại đế A-dục chỉ ân sủng người vợ trẻ nhất của mình, là Tishyaraksha.

"*Người ta nói rằng thiếp Tishyaraksha có một đứa con trai với vua là Kunala, nhiếp chính ở Takshashila và là người thừa kế ngai vàng, nhưng thái tử đã bị một mưu kế quỷ quyệt tạo phản khiến Thái tử Kunala bị tội oan. Những kẻ hành quyết chính thức đã tha cho thái tử Kunala và anh ta trở thành một ca sĩ lang thang đi cùng với người vợ yêu quý của mình,là Kanchanmala. Tại Pataliputra,*

Đại đế A-dục đã nghe bài hát của Kunala, và nhận ra rằng sự bất hạnh của Kunala có thể là sự trừng phạt cho một quá khứ nào đó tội lỗi của chính hoàng đế. Vua kết án tử hình Thiếp Tishyaraksha, phục hồi Kunala với chức vị trong triều đình.

Trong Ashokavadana, miêu tả là thái tử Kunala đã tha thứ cho mẹ Tishyaraksha, bởi thái tử đã được giác ngộ thông qua việc tu tập Phật pháp. Thái tử cũng lạy xin Vua A-dục hãy tha thứ cho Bà ấy. tiếp theo hoàng tử Samprati, thái tử Kunala được kế vị cai trị trong năm mươi năm cho đến khi thăng hà."[102]

Đại đế A-dục là một bộ phim lịch sử với sử thi chính bằng tiếng Hindi của Ấn Độ từ năm 2001, trong đó ngôi sao nổi tiếng, Shah Rukh Khan, đóng vai Vua Aśoka với nữ diễn viên Kareena Kapoor đóng vai vợ của ông. Bộ phim mô tả rằng Hoàng đế Aśoka là một trong những nhà cải cách đạo đức vĩ đại trong lịch sử văn minh, là người tiên phong sớm về các giá trị nhân đạo trong cai trị đất nước.

---

102. B.R. Bandarkar, *Ashoka* (Kolkata: Calcutta University, 1999), 87, 89.

Hơn hai nghìn sáu trăm năm trôi qua, những đóng góp của vua Ashoka vẫn có ảnh hưởng mạnh mẽ đến đời sống của người dân Ấn Độ nói riêng và Phật giáo nói chung.

Đáng chú ý nhất là quốc huy và quốc kỳ của Ấn Độ, cột đá và bánh xe Pháp ở Vườn Nai, Sarnath, Varanasi, Ấn Độ của vua Ashoka, vẫn là biểu tượng quen thuộc với người dân.

Vua A-dục là một đệ tử Phật, một Phật tử thuần thành, một quân vương hộ trì Phật Pháp, lấy giới luật (Thập thiện) và lục hòa để trị dân, với mục đích khiến quần chúng quy ngưỡng về con đường lành, tu tập, giác ngộ và giải thoát. Nhờ công đức hộ trì mạnh mẽ này, bánh xe Pháp đã đang và sẽ lăn mãi để mang ánh sáng từ bi và trí tuệ của Đức Phật đến cho mọi người ở mọi nơi trên thế giới.

IV. LỊCH SỬ PHẬT GIÁO VIỆT NAM

4.1. Những vết ích đầu tiên của con người

Các cuộc khai quật khảo cổ học đã tiết lộ sự tồn tại của con người ở Việt Nam ngày nay ngay từ thời kỳ đồ đá cũ. "*Hóa thạch Homo erectus có niên đại khoảng 500.000 năm trước Công nguyên đã được tìm thấy trong các hang động ở tỉnh Lạng Sơn và Nghệ An ở miền bắc Việt Nam.*"[103]

4.2. Từ Paleolithic đến Neolithic

Đến khoảng năm 1000 TCN, sự phát triển của nghề trồng lúa nước và nghề đúc đồng ở vùng đồng bằng sông Mã và sông Hồng đã dẫn đến sự hưng thịnh của văn hóa Đông Sơn, nổi bật với những chiếc trống đồng tinh xảo. Vào thời điểm này, "*Nhà nước Văn Lang và Âu Lạc thời*

103. https://www.indochinavalue.com/Vietnam-travel-guide/Vietnamese
-history/prehistoric-Vietnam;
https://giaoduc.net.vn/ten-goi-viet-nam-co-tu-khi-nao-post189425.gd

kì đầu của Việt Nam đã xuất hiện, và ảnh hưởng của nền văn hóa này đã lan sang các khu vực khác của Đông Nam Á, bao gồm cả Đông Nam Á trên biển trong suốt thiên niên kỷ thứ nhất trước Công nguyên."[104] Con người xuất hiện ở Việt Nam cách đây khoảng 10.000–30.000 năm trước với dấu tích Núi Đọ, Thần Sa, Sơn Vi. Thời đại mới tiêu biểu với các nền văn hóa Hòa Bình, Bắc Sơn cách đây khoảng 6.000-10.000 năm và thời đại kim khí cách đây khoảng 4.000 năm.

4.3. Quốc hiệu Việt Nam

Kinh Dương Vương là thỉ tổ của dân tộc Việt Nam. Nước Văn Lang tồn tại gần 2000 năm, trải qua 18 đời vua Hùng, kinh đô đặt ở Phong Châu. Nhà Thục (257–208 TCN) lấy tên nước là Âu Lạc, đóng đô ở Cổ Loa. Nhà Triệu (207–111 TCN) chiếm Âu Lạc, đổi quốc hiệu là Nam Việt. Nhà Hán vào năm (111 TCN–39) chiếm Nam Việt, đổi tên là Giao Chỉ. "Việt Nam", là quốc hiệu của Việt Nam chính thức xuất hiện từ thời nhà Nguyễn, được tuyên bố vào năm 1804. Khi Cách mạng Tháng Tám năm 1945 thành công vào ngày 2 tháng 9 năm 1945, khi "Chủ tịch Hồ Chí Minh đọc Tuyên ngôn Độc lập khai sinh ra Nhà nước Dân chủ Việt Nam Cộng hòa (Việt Nam Dân chủ Cộng hòa), quốc hiệu Việt Nam đã được chính thức công nhận."

Việt Nam là một phần của Đế quốc Trung Quốc, từ năm 111 trước Công nguyên đến năm 939 sau Công nguyên, trong hơn một thiên niên kỷ. Nhà nước Việt Nam độc lập được thành lập vào năm 939, sau chiến thắng của Việt Nam trong trận sông Bạch Đằng. Các triều đại hoàng gia Việt Nam nối tiếp nhau phát triển rực rỡ khi đất nước

---

104. Nguyễn Lang (aka Zen Master Thích Nhất Hạnh), Việt Nam Phật giáo Sử luận, tập 1,2,3. 1973.
https://langmai.org/tang-kinh-cac/vien-sach/giang-kinh/viet-nam-phat-giao-su-luan/chuong-12-tran-nhan-tong-va-thien-phai-truc-lam/

mở rộng về mặt địa lý và chính trị vào Đông Nam Á cho đến khi bán đảo Đông Dương bị Pháp đô hộ vào giữa thế kỷ XIX.

Sau sự chiếm đóng của Nhật Bản vào những năm 1940, người Việt Nam đã chiến đấu chống lại sự cai trị của Pháp trong Chiến tranh Đông Dương lần thứ nhất, cuối cùng đã đánh đuổi quân Pháp vào năm 1954. Sau đó, Việt Nam bị chia cắt về mặt chính trị thành hai miền đối nghịch nhau, là miền Bắc và miền Nam của Việt Nam. Xung đột giữa hai bên gia tăng dữ dội được gọi là Chiến tranh Việt Nam. Chiến tranh kết thúc với chiến thắng của Bắc Việt năm 1975.

Việt Nam đã thống nhất nhưng vẫn nghèo khó và bị cô lập về chính trị. Năm 1986, Việt Nam tiến hành đổi mới kinh tế, đổi mới chính sách đối ngoại với phương châm muốn làm bạn với tất cả các nước. Nhờ đó, kinh tế, chính trị, xã hội Việt Nam ngày càng ổn định và phát triển. Hiện nay, đất nước Việt Nam đang được hưởng hòa bình sau một quá trình lịch sử đấu tranh dựng nước và giữ nước lâu dài.

4.4. Phật giáo Việt Nam

Đạo Phật ở Việt Nam (trong tiếng Việt gọi là đạo Phật

hay Phật giáo) do người dân tộc Việt Nam thực hành, chủ yếu theo truyền thống Đại thừa (Bắc Tông). Phật giáo có thể đã đến Việt Nam lần đầu tiên vào thế kỷ thứ ba hoặc thứ hai trước Công nguyên từ Nam Á hoặc từ Trung Quốc vào thế kỷ thứ nhất hoặc thứ hai sau Công nguyên. Phật giáo Việt Nam có quan hệ cộng sinh với một số yếu tố Đạo giáo, tâm linh Trung Hoa và tín ngưỡng dân gian Việt Nam.

Thủ tướng Ấn Độ N. D. Modi thăm chùa Quán Sứ, Hà Nội, 2016

Có nhiều giả thuyết mâu thuẫn nhau về việc Phật giáo đến Việt Nam lần đầu tiên vào thế kỷ thứ ba hoặc thứ hai trước Công nguyên thông qua các phái đoàn từ Ấn Độ, hay trong thế kỷ thứ nhất hoặc thứ hai sang từ Trung Quốc. Trong cả hai trường hợp, vào cuối thế kỷ thứ hai sau Công nguyên, Việt Nam đã phát triển thành một trung tâm Phật giáo Đại thừa lớn của khu vực với trung tâm tên là Luy Lâu thuộc tỉnh Bắc Ninh, phía Đông bắc thủ đô Hà Nội ngày nay. Luy Lâu là thủ phủ của vùng Giao Chỉ (Giao Chỉ) nhà Hán và là một địa điểm nổi tiếng được nhiều nhà sư truyền giáo Phật giáo Ấn Độ viếng thăm trên đường đến Trung Quốc. *Các nhà sư đi theo "con đường thương mại tơ lụa hàng hải từ tiểu lục địa Ấn Độ đến Trung Quốc với các thương nhân Ấn Độ. Một số kinh điển Đại thừa và kinh tạng đã được dịch sang tiếng Hán cổ ở đó, bao gồm Kinh Tứ Thập Nhị Chương và Kinh Quán niệm hơi thở.*"[105]

Trong mười tám thế kỷ tiếp theo, Việt Nam và Trung Quốc đã có nhiều đặc điểm chung về di sản văn hóa, triết học và tôn giáo. Điều này là do sự gần gũi về địa lý và Việt Nam đã bị Trung Quốc đô hộ hai lần. Vì thế, nói chung Phật giáo Việt Nam có quan hệ với Phật giáo Trung Quốc ở một mức độ nào đó ảnh hưởng sự hình thành của Phật giáo Trung Quốc sau thời nhà Tống.

Mặt khác, Phật giáo Nguyên thủy có thể đã được kết hợp chặt chẽ thống nhất thông qua sự thôn tính phía Nam của người Khmer và các vùng lãnh thổ. Vào thời nhà Đinh (968–980), Phật giáo được nhà nước công nhận là một tín ngưỡng chính thức (971), thể hiện sự coi trọng tín ngưỡng Phật giáo của các vị vua Việt Nam.

Nhà Tiền Lê (980–1009) cũng dành sự công nhận tương tự cho giáo hội Phật giáo. Sự phát triển của Phật giáo trong thời gian này được cho là nhờ việc hỗ trợ của các nhà sư uyên bác vào triều đình vì quốc gia mới độc lập cần một cơ sở tôn giáo để xây dựng đất nước. Sau đó, vai trò này được nhường lại cho Nho giáo. Phật giáo Việt Nam đạt đến đỉnh cao vào thời nhà Lý (1009–1225) bắt đầu với nhà sáng lập Lý Thái Tổ, người được nuôi dưỡng trong một ngôi chùa. Các vua thời Lý đều tôn Phật giáo là quốc giáo. Điều này tồn tại với "*thời nhà Trần (1225–1400) nhưng Phật giáo phải chia sẻ giai đoạn với sự phát triển mới nổi lên của Nho giáo*".

Đến thế kỷ XV, Phật giáo không còn được triều đình hậu Lê ưa chuộng, mặc dù vẫn còn phổ biến trong quần chúng. Các quan chức như Lê Quát đã phê phán đây là dị giáo và lãng phí. Mãi đến thế kỷ 19, Phật giáo mới lấy lại

105. Lê Văn Hưu, Phan Phu Tiên, Ngô Sĩ Liên. Đại Việt Sử Ký Toàn Thư (National Bureau for Historical Records). 1993, P. 182. Viện Khoa Học Xã Hội Việt Nam dịch (1985–1992).

được tầm vóc dưới thời nhà Nguyễn, được sự ủng hộ của hoàng gia.

Thiền phái do vua Trần Nhân Tông (1258–1308) sáng lập, được đặt tên là Trúc Lâm (nghĩa là Thiền phái "Rừng tre"). Điều này cho thấy ảnh hưởng sâu sắc của triết học Nho giáo và Đạo giáo. Tuy nhiên, uy tín của Trúc Lâm suy yếu trong những thế kỷ tiếp theo khi Nho giáo trở nên thống trị trong triều đình. Vào thế kỷ XVII, một nhóm nhà sư Trung Quốc, đứng đầu là thiền sư Nguyên Thiều, đã giới thiệu trường phái "Ling" (Lâm Tế). Một nhánh thuần hóa hơn của Lâm Tế là trường phái Liễu Quán được thành lập vào thế kỷ 18 và từ đó trở thành một nhánh của Thiền Việt Nam. Từ thế kỷ XX và XXI, Thiền sư Thích Thanh Từ đã khôi phục Thiền phái Trúc Lâm bằng việc thành lập hàng trăm thiền viện Trúc Lâm trong và ngoài nước, đặc biệt là núi Yên Tử (Quảng Ninh) nơi Tổ sư Trần Nhân Tông tọa lạc, trú trì và truyền bá Thiền tông Việt Nam.

Phật giáo có mặt ở Việt Nam hơn 2600 năm, gắn liền với những bước thăng trầm của vận mệnh dân tộc, từ thời Hùng Vương, Chử Đồng Tử – Tiên Dung, Hai Bà Trưng, Ngô Quyền, nhà Lý (1010–1225), Nhà Trần (1225–1400), Nhà Lê (1418–1527), Trịnh-Nguyễn (1533–1788), Nhà Nguyễn (1802–1883), Pháp đô hộ (1883–1945) và tiếp cho đến ngày nay. Đạo Phật với đạo lý làm lành lánh dữ, giữ tâm thanh tịnh vẫn tồn tại trong lòng dân tộc như nhà thơ Huyền Không đã nói:

Mái chùa che chở hồn dân tộc

Nếp sống muôn đời của tổ tiên.

(Nhớ Chùa của Huyền Không)

Đặc biệt qua các triều đại của Nhà Đinh, Lê, Lý, Trần, Trịnh, Nguyễn... Phật giáo phát triển đến đỉnh cao,

---

https://www.tuvienquangduc.com.au/lichsu/lichsuVietnam/Daivietsukytoanthu.pdf

nhiều nhà sư đã trở thành Quốc sư cho các Vua Việt Nam, cố vấn và hoạch định các chương trình phát triển quốc gia như Hòa thượng Khuông Việt, Tăng Thống của Tăng đoàn. Ngô Chân Lưu, Thiền sư Vạn Hạnh, Thiền sư Tuệ Trung Thượng. Sỹ, vua Trần Thái Tông, Tổ sư Thiền phái Trúc Lâm – vua Trần Nhân Tông, v.v.

V. HOÀNG ĐẾ TRẦN NHÂN TÔNG (1258–1308)

5.1. Từ thuở nhỏ đã có Thánh tướng như đức Phật Hoàng

Phật Hoàng Trần Nhân Tông, Sơ Tổ Thiền Phái Trúc Lâm

"Trần Nhân Tông, vị hoàng đế thứ ba nhà Trần của Việt Nam, sinh ngày 7 tháng 12 năm 1258 (11 tháng 11 năm Mậu Ngọ). Tên khai sinh là Trần Khâm. Ngài là con đầu của vua Trần Thánh Tông."[106]

106. Việt Nam Phật Giáo Sử Luận (*History of Vietnamese Buddhism*),

"Người ta nói rằng Trần Khâm mới sinh ra đã có những dấu hiệu ưu tú của thánh nhân, chẳng hạn như thể chất vàng ròng và phong thái sáng sủa hoàn hảo. Cả hai dấu hiệu được coi là dấu hiệu của một sự xuất hiện phi thường trên trời. Ông nội là Thái Tông và cha là Thánh Tông phong cho ông là "Kim Tiên Đồng Tử."[107] Nhờ những tướng tốt này mà vua còn được tôn là "Phật Hoàng" tức Phật Hoàng Trần Nhân Tông từ khi Ngài còn nhỏ.

5.2. Ngài muốn từ bỏ ngôi vị vua để trở thành bậc ẩn sĩ

"Hoàng tử Trần Khâm được phong làm thái tử nhà Trần vào tháng 12 năm 1274 (16 tuổi). Bản thân Hoàng đế cũng đã sáng tác các bài thơ và một tác phẩm văn học có tên là Di hậu lục (Hai cuốn sách). Ông đã dạy thái tử cách ứng xử để chuẩn bị cho vị vua tương lai và đức tin, vì vậy thái tử trở thành một bậc thầy của Tam giáo (Phật giáo, Đạo giáo và Nho giáo). Tuy nhiên, Trần Khâm thích đời sống thiền môn Phật giáo và đã theo học Thiền từ khi còn nhỏ. Năm mười sáu tuổi, ông được phong làm thái tử. Ông cố "nhường ngôi cho em nhưng vua cha Trần Thánh Tông không chịu."[108]

Vua Trần Thánh Tông chọn quận chúa Quyên Thanh là con gái của Hưng Đạo Vương và Công chúa Thiên Thành (sau được tôn là Nguyên Từ Quốc mẫu) làm vợ của Trần Khâm. Trong hoàng cung cùng vợ, Trần Khâm sống trong

---

tập 1,2,3. Nguyễn Lang (aka Zen Master Thích Nhất Hạnh), Lá Bối. 1973; https://langmai.org/tang-kinh-cac/vien-sach/giang-kinh/viet-nam-phat-giao-su-luan/chuong-12-tran- nhan-tong-va-thien-phai-truc-lam/

107. Book *Tam Tổ Thực Lục* called "The Golden Buddha" (Phật Hoàng). Ibid. https://langmai.org/tang kinh- cac/vien-sach/giang-kinh/viet-nam-phat-giao-su-luan/chuong-12-tran-nhan-tong-va-thien-phai-truc-lam/

108. Lê Văn Hưu, Phan Phu Tiên, Ngô Sĩ Liên, 1993. 18.

sung sướng an nhàn nhưng luôn nghĩ đến việc sống đời khổ hạnh bằng cách xuất gia. Đây cũng chính là mối ưu tư mà thái tử Sĩ-đạt-đa (Siddharta) đã muốn có một cuộc đời giải thoát, không bị ràng buộc, nên Thái tử Sĩ-đạt-đa rời cung điện hoàng gia tìm kiếm chân lý vào lúc nửa đêm của một ngày trăng tròn, để lại người vợ là công nương Da-du (Yasodhara) và đứa con là thái tử La-hầu-la (Rahula). Đây được gọi là sự từ bỏ vĩ đại. Vị hoàng tử này sau này trở thành Đức Phật Thích Ca Mâu Ni, Đấng Giác Ngộ.

Trần Nhân Tông cũng vậy, đã có một cuộc từ bỏ vĩ đại, "*Một đêm vào giờ Tý, trèo ra khỏi thành quách, từ bỏ những phú quý địa vị nhất cuộc đời, trốn đến núi Yên Tử. Ở đó, Ông đến gần chùa Tháp ở núi Đông Cửu. Trời vừa sáng, liền trốn vào trong tháp nằm nghỉ.*"[109]

Vị sư trụ trì của ngôi chùa đã làm một bữa ăn cho vị khách vì người khách lạ có ngoại hình phi phàm khác thường. Vị sư trưởng đã nhận ra Ngài và gửi tin nhắn cho nhà vua. Đội quân do nhà vua triển khai đã tìm được Ông và bắt Ông trở về cung điện, Do vậy, vì thương cha và vì nghĩa nặng với nước, thái tử đã trở về với cuộc sống trần gian để nối dõi tông đường.

5.3. Dù là Vua, Ngài vẫn Ăn Chay và Tu Thiền

Năm 21 tuổi (năm 1279), Ngài lên ngôi hoàng đế, hiệu là Trần Nhân Tông. Tuy ở địa vị cao sang nhưng Ngài vẫn giữ mình thanh tịnh, ăn chay, mỗi ngày ăn một bữa vào buổi trưa và thường đến chùa Từ Phước tu tập.

Vào năm xuất gia, vua mời Văn Túc vương Đạo Tái (con Trần Quang Khải) cùng dùng bữa. Rất mến Văn Túc vương Đạo Tái, nhà vua mời Đạo Tái đến thăm lầu Dưỡng Đức ở điện Thánh Từ, sai người bưng mâm cơm mời Đạo Tái. Nhà vua vốn là người ăn chay nên chỉ ngồi nhìn Đạo Tái ăn bữa cơm không chay. Nhà vua viết bài thơ sau:

---

109. Lê Văn Hưu, Phan Phu Tiên, Ngô Sĩ Liên, 1993. 195

Món quy cước đỏ thắm
Món mã yên vàng thơm
Sơn tăng giữ tịnh giới
Cùng ngồi không cùng ăn.[110]

Ngay cả khi nhà vua chưa xuất gia, Ông vẫn tự coi mình là một "nhà sư trên núi". Ngài ấp ủ ý nguyện xuất gia và chuẩn bị cho việc xuất gia của mình.

Có một sự kiện quan trọng khác trong cuộc đời Ngài. Một hôm, trong lúc nghỉ trưa, Ngài nằm mơ thấy trong rốn mình mọc ra một hoa sen vàng to bằng bánh xe, trên đó có một vị Phật bằng vàng. Có người đứng bên cạnh nói: "Ông có biết vị Phật này không? Đó là sự chuyển hóa đức hạnh!". Tỉnh dậy, ông đem việc ấy dâng lên vua cha là vua Thánh Tông, vua khóc và khuyên con nên ở đời vương giả, hoãn lại việc xuất gia như sau:

Sách "*Tam Tổ Thực Lục*"[111] có ghi: "*Tuy ngồi trên chín tầng đài vinh quang, nhưng cuộc đời Ngài rất trong sạch. Một hôm ngủ trưa ở chùa Từ Phước trong nội thành, vua Trần Nhân Tông nằm mộng thấy trên rốn mình mọc hoa sen to bằng bánh xe, trên có tượng Phật bằng vàng. Bên cạnh có người chỉ nhà vua hỏi: Ngài có biết vị Phật này không? Đó chính là chuyển hóa đức hạnh! Vua tỉnh dậy, đem giấc mộng thuật lại với vua Thánh Tông, ai nấy đều kinh ngạc. Kể từ đó, ông thường xuyên ăn chay tránh thịt cá, khuôn mặt hốc hác. Thánh Tông thấy người con còn nuôi ý muốn xuất gia, khóc mà nói: 'Cha già rồi, chỉ trông*

110. Việt Nam Phật Giáo Sử Luận (*History of Vietnam Buddhism*), tập 1,2,3. Nguyễn Lang (aka Zen Master Thích Nhất Hạnh), Lá Bối. 1973. https://langmai.org/tang-kinh-cac/vien-sach/giang-kinh/viet-nam-phat-giao-su-luan/chuong-12 tran- nhan-tong-va-thien-phai-truc-lam/

111. Việt Nam Phật Giáo Sử Luận (*History of Vietnamese Buddhism*), tập 1,2,3. Nguyễn Lang (aka Zen Master Thích Nhất Hạnh), Lá Bối. 1973. https://langmai.org/tang-kinh-cac/vien-sach/giang-kinh/viet-nam-phat-giao-su-luan/chuong-12-tran-nhan-tong-va-thien-phai-truc-lam

cậy vào một mình con, nếu con còn như thế, làm sao nối được cơ nghiệp của tổ tông?'. Vua Trần Nhân Tông cũng vậy. đã khóc, và ông chấp nhận giữ ngai vàng trong khi *học Phật pháp.*"[112]

Ông là người từ bi, sáng suốt và đa tài, đọc đủ loại kinh điển từ nội học và ngoại học, thường mời các bậc thầy Phật giáo đến giảng về Thiền học. Ông cũng từng tham kiến với Tuệ Trung Thượng Sĩ, nhờ đó mà thâm nhập được tinh túy của Thiền nên thường lấy thân phận đệ tử khiêm nhường coi Ngài Tuệ Trung là thầy của mình.

5.4. Ba lần đánh giặc Nguyên-Mông để bảo vệ đất nước

Hoàng đế Trần Nhân Tông và cha của ông, Thượng hoàng Trần Thánh Tông, được ghi nhận là những vị chỉ huy tối cao đã lãnh đạo Nhà Trần ba lần chiến thắng quân xâm lược Mông Cổ (Mông) và Nguyên (quân Nguyên) của Trung Quốc, thiết lập một thời kỳ hòa bình lâu dài và thịnh vượng trên cả nước.

Đầu tiên, quân Mông Cổ tấn công Đại Việt vào tháng 2 năm 1258. Từ Đại Lý, khoảng 15.000–25.000 kỵ binh Mông Cổ và 20.000 quân Đại Lý (tổng cộng khoảng 35.000–45.000 người) tiến vào Đại Việt.

Thứ hai, hai mươi bảy năm sau, Hoàng đế nhà Nguyên Hốt Tất Liệt hạ lệnh xâm lược Đại Việt. Cuộc chiến này kéo dài từ cuối tháng Chạp năm Bính Thân đến hết tháng Tư năm Đinh Dậu (cuối tháng Giêng đến cuối tháng 5 năm 1285 Dương lịch). Lần này, quân Nguyên chuẩn bị cho cuộc chiến tốt hơn, huy động một lực lượng lớn hơn nhiều, lên tới hàng vạn quân. Ngoài quân từ phía Bắc xuống, còn có thủy quân từ mặt trận Chiêm Thành ở phía Nam đến hỗ trợ.

112. Ibid

Thứ ba, ngay sau thất bại, trao trả Trung Quốc năm 1287, quân Nguyên đã chấn chỉnh, bổ sung lực lượng để phục thù. Rút kinh nghiệm trước những thất bại, quân Nguyên đóng nhiều thuyền lương thực vượt biển để quay lại đánh Đại Việt lần thứ ba. Cuộc chiến này kéo dài khoảng bốn tháng, từ cuối tháng 12 năm 1287 đến cuối tháng 4 năm 1288.

Khi bắt đầu cuộc chiến, Thượng Hoàng Thánh Tông và Nhân Tông phải ra lệnh cho quân thiện chiến rút lui để tránh áp lực từ quân Nguyên khi Thái tử Chiêu Minh Trần Quang Khải chỉ huy quân đội cố gắng ngăn chặn hạm đội của Sogetu ở tỉnh Nghệ An. Trong thời gian này, có một số quan đại thần và thành viên hoàng tộc nhà Trần đã đào thoát sang phe Nguyên, trong đó có anh trai của Thánh Tông, Hoàng tử Chiêu Quốc Trần Ích Tắc và Trần Kiện, con trai của Hoàng tử Tĩnh Quốc Trần Quốc Khang.

"Đối phó với mối đe dọa từ phương bắc, tháng 10 năm 1282, Thượng hoàng Trần Thánh Tông và Vua Trần Nhân Tông triệu tập các thành viên hoàng tộc và các quan trong triều để bàn về cuộc chiến không thể tránh khỏi. Năm 1283, Hưng Đạo Vương (tên thật là Trần Quốc Tuấn) được phong làm "Tổng tư lệnh (Quốc công Tiết Chế) Quân đội Đại Việt, Thượng hoàng và hoàng đế bắt đầu tập trận với các tướng lĩnh và quân đội của họ."[113]

Để xây dựng cả nước thành một quốc gia kháng chiến mạnh mẽ, hoàng đế đã lắng nghe ý kiến của những người có kinh nghiệm. Ông mở hội nghị các tướng lĩnh ở Bình Than sau đó là hội nghị các bậc hiền sĩ ở Diên Hồng. Chẳng hạn, theo ý tưởng khôn khéo của vua Nhân Tông, "Mùa Đông, tháng 10, năm Bính Ngọ (1282), vua Nhân Tông đi Bình Than, ở lại làng Trần Xá, yết kiến triều đình và trăm các quan, phải bàn kế khéo léo, chia nhau khôn ngoan giữ những nơi nguy hiểm.

"Cuộc xâm lược đầu tiên của người Mông Cổ chỉ là

113. Lê Văn Hưu, Phan Phu Tiên, Ngô Sĩ Liên. 1993. 195.

ném đá. Tuy bị nhà Trần đập tan nhưng hiểm họa lớn nhất vẫn còn đó. Ba mươi năm sau, đội quân xâm lược khổng lồ cả trên bộ lẫn dưới nước của đế quốc Nguyên Mông, cực thịnh sau khi đánh đổ nhà Nam Tống, đã tiến vào nước ta với khí thế khôn lường, chúng ta không thể chống cự. Tuy nhiên, lòng nhân từ của Thiền sư Nhân Tông không muốn làm vua đã cùng với đội quân ít ỏi của mình đã bình tĩnh đánh bại đội quân "thần thịnh nộ" của Trung Quốc và Mông Cổ."[114]

Ngày 10 tháng 5 âm lịch năm Ất Dậu (1285), Trần Quang Khải đánh trận quyết định ở Chương Dương, thủy quân của Sogetu gần như bị tiêu diệt, cán cân chiến trường nghiêng hẳn về nhà Trần. Mười ngày sau khi Tướng Sogetu bị giết, Thượng hoàng Thánh tông và Vua Nhân Tông trở về kinh đô Thăng Long vào ngày 6 tháng 6 năm Ất Dậu (1285).

Tháng 3 năm 1287, nhà Nguyên mở cuộc xâm lược Đại Việt lần thứ ba. Khác với lần tấn công thứ hai, lần này Tổng tư lệnh Hưng Đạo Vương (Trần Quốc Tuấn) khẳng định với hoàng đế rằng quân Đại Việt có thể dễ dàng bẻ gãy chiến dịch quân sự của quân Nguyên. Thật vậy, cuộc xâm lược này đã kết thúc một năm sau đó bằng thất bại thảm hại của hải quân nhà Nguyên trong trận Bạch Đằng vào ngày 8 tháng 3 năm Mậu Tý (1288).

Ngoài Trần Quốc Tuấn, một danh tướng khác của nhà Trần trong thời gian này là Nhân Huệ Vương (Trần Khánh Dư) người đã tiêu diệt đoàn thuyền hậu cần của quân Nguyên trong trận Vân Đồn hay tướng quân Phạm Ngũ Lão, người cầm quân phục kích quân rút lui của Thái tử Toghan.

Tình thế nguy cấp của nhà Trần bắt đầu thay đổi sau chiến thắng trong trận Hàm Tử vào tháng 4 năm 1285, nơi quân đội do Trần Nhật Duật, Hoàng tử Chiêu Thành, Trần Quốc Toản và Nguyễn Khoái chỉ huy cuối cùng đã đánh

114. https://vi.wikipedia.org/wiki/Chi%E1%BA%BFn_tranh_Nguyen-Mong

bại được hạm đội của Sogetu. Khi khen thưởng các tướng lĩnh và quan lại nhà Trần sau chiến thắng, "*Thánh Tông và Nhân Tông cũng nhắc nhở họ phải đề phòng biên giới phía Bắc*".[115]

Cuộc chiến Nguyên Mông—Đại Việt hay Kháng chiến chống quân xâm lược Nguyên Mông là cuộc chiến bảo vệ Tổ quốc của quân dân Đại Việt thời kỳ đầu nhà Trần dưới thời các vua Trần Thánh Tông và Trần Nhân Tông. Tuy thời gian kháng chiến kéo dài từ năm 1258 đến năm 1288, nhưng thời gian chính thức chỉ kéo dài khoảng 9 tháng, chia làm ba giai đoạn I, II và III, là thời gian chủ động ngoại giao. Vì vậy, ba cuộc kháng chiến này được ghi trong những trang lịch sử hào hùng nhất của dân tộc Việt Nam chiến công tiêu biểu của nhà Trần.

Từ xưa đến nay có thể nói Vua Nhân Tông là một bậc chân tu theo đạo Phật, có tấm lòng từ bi rộng lớn và cũng là một bậc anh hùng sáng suốt trong lịch sử Việt Nam. Không chỉ cai quản đất nước hùng mạnh, đánh tan hai cuộc xâm lược của đạo quân Mông Cổ khủng khiếp nhất thế giới, Ngài còn mở mang bờ cõi hai châu cho Việt Nam cũng như đi sâu vào đời sống tâm linh.

115. Chapuis, 1995. 84–85. 32, Ngô Sĩ Liên. 1993. 19.

5.5. Vua Trần Nhân Tông xuất gia, sáng lập Thiền Phái Trúc Lâm

Năm 1293, Trần Nhân Tông nhường ngôi cho con là Trần Anh Tông và dìu dắt tân vương trong 6 năm. Năm 1299, Ngài xuất gia tại Ngọa Vân Am, trong rừng trúc trên núi Yên Tử, nghiêm trì mười hai giới khổ hạnh, nên Ngài được tôn xưng là "Đại ẩn sĩ Vân Hương" (nghĩa là Hương Vân Đại Đầu Đà)" tức là người giữ giới,"

"*Sau khi xuất gia một thời gian, Hương Vân Đại Đầu Đà thành lập Thiền phái Trúc Lâm trên núi Yên Tử. Đây là ngôi Tu viện Phật giáo bản địa duy nhất ở Việt Nam chịu ảnh hưởng triết học Nho giáo và Lão giáo. Đây là một phương pháp Thiền Phật giáo nhập thế, vì Ngài còn tham chính triều đình mà vẫn duy trì việc tu hành (đồng thời là thế tục và siêu thế). Ngài đã trở thành vị Tổ thứ sáu của phái Yên Tử, là vị tổ thứ nhất của Thiền phái Trúc Lâm. Ngài còn có các tên gọi khác như Trúc Lâm bậc Đại Sĩ (Trúc Lâm Đại Đầu Đà), Trúc Lâm Đại Sĩ và Phật Hoàng Điều Ngự (Giác Hoàng Điều Ngự)*".[116]

Toàn quang cảnh nơi ra đời của Thiền Phái Trúc Lâm, Núi Yên Tử, Quảng Ninh

116. Ibid

Ở núi Yên Tử, Ngài mở Tịnh xá, thuyết pháp cho người xuất gia, thu nhận được khá nhiều đệ tử.

Phật giáo Trúc Lâm đóng vai trò là Phật giáo nhập thế, gắn bó mật thiết với chính trị, văn hóa và xã hội. Thiền phái Trúc Lâm rất thích hợp với phong trào này, đó là lý do chính mà Thiền phái này được thành lập. Truyền thống Phật giáo Yên Tử và sự xuất hiện của Trúc Lâm đã mang nhiều tính chất xã hội nhập thế, nên việc dùng một danh hiệu mới cho thiền phái mới ở Việt Nam thế kỷ XIV là điều đương nhiên và hợp lý.

Vào thế kỷ VI-XIII, nước Đại Việt tồn tại chủ yếu dựa trên ba dòng Thiền Tỳ-Ni-Đa-Lưu-Chi (Vinītaruci)[117] Vô Ngôn Thông[118] và Thảo Đường."[119]

---

117. In the sixth century, the Patriarch Vinītaruci went from India to China to study Buddhism with the Patriarch Tăng Xán. After attaining enlightenment, he was taught by the Patriarch Tăng Xán to go to the South to spread Zen Buddhism, so he went to Vietnam to stay at Dâu Pagoda.

118. In the ninth century, there was Zen Master Vô Ngôn Thôn, a disciple of Bá Trượng's ancestor in China who went to Vietnam to transmit meditation, so there was Vô Ngôn Thôn Zen Sect.

119. There was Master Thảo Đường, who, when the Ly Dynasty conquered Champa, captured a number of officials and brought them back to Vietnam. Only in Thăng Long did he discover that he was a Zen

Thái tử Trần Khâm, tức vua Trần Nhân Tông sau này, được vua Trần Thánh Tông cử đi học đạo đức với Tuệ Trung Thượng Sĩ. Trước khi trở về cung, hoàng tử hỏi: "Mục tiêu chính của thiền định là gì?" Tuệ Trung Thượng Sĩ đáp: "Tự xét mình là chính, tránh chạy ra ngoài", tức là quay lại soi mình, đó là bổn phận chính để đạt giác ngộ, không gì khác, không phải từ bên ngoài.

Sau khi lên ngôi, vua Trần Nhân Tông vừa lo việc trị nước, vừa lo nghiên cứu kinh điển Phật giáo không lúc nào lơ là. Lên ngôi một thời gian, thấy đã có người thừa kế, bốn mươi mốt tuổi, giao hết quyền hành cho con rồi xuất gia. Ngài lên núi Yên Tử tu hành. Sau năm năm tu khổ hạnh trong rừng trúc, Ngài hoàn toàn giác ngộ về Đạo. Từ đó, Ngài truyền bá và thành lập Thiền phái Trúc Lâm Yên Tử.

"*Thiền phái Trúc Lâm Yên Tử ra đời, kết tụ ba tinh hoa của ba thiền phái Tỳ-Ni-Đa-Lưu-Chi, Vô Ngôn Thông, Thảo Đường, kết tụ thành một Thiền phái thuần Việt.*"[120] Từ khi thiền phái Trúc Lâm Yên Tử ra đời, các thiền phái khác đều vắng bóng và không còn phát triển. Đây được xem là Giáo Hội Phật Giáo Thống Nhất đầu tiên ở Việt Nam.

"*Thiền phái Trúc Lâm tiếp thu "nền tảng của Phật giáo Nam Á và thiền Đông Độ (Ấn Độ) đồng thời sử dụng các giá trị văn hóa Việt Nam, khuyến khích Phật tử đóng góp cho xã hội dựa trên lòng từ bi và trí tuệ của Phật giáo. Bản thân thiền sư Trúc Lâm không chỉ tu ở Yên Tử mà còn hoằng pháp ở nhiều chùa như Phổ Minh (Thiên Trường), Sùng Nghiêm (Chí Linh), Vĩnh Nghiêm (Yên Dũng) và Báo*

master, since then the kings and mandarins of the Lý Dynasty admired and respected him and he became the Patriarch of the Thảo Đường Zen sect in Vietnam.

120. http://thuongchieu.net/index.php/phapthoai/suong/1960-pht-giao-thin-tong-vit-nam

Ân – Siêu Loại (nay thuộc Gia Lâm, Hà Nội)."[121]

5.6. Hình thành một Xã Hội Phật giáo

Để ủng hộ đất nước Đại Việt và tìm hiểu kinh điển của Đức Phật, vào tháng 2 âm lịch năm 1295, Thiền sư Trúc Lâm đã cử các quan ngoại giao Trần Khắc Dụng và Phạm Thảo sang nhà Nguyên thỉnh Đại Tạng Kinh (Kinh, Luật, và Luận). Yêu cầu này được Nguyên Thành Tông chấp thuận. Kinh do sứ bộ đem về cất giữ ở điện Thiên Trường, ngoài ra vua còn cho in bản để lưu hành trong nước.

Năm 1304, Hương Vân Đại Sư Đại Đầu Đà (Trần Nhân Tông) đi khắp nước khuyên dân bỏ thờ dâm thần, bỏ tà kiến. Ngài dạy mười điều thiện, (1*) không sát sinh, (2) không trộm cắp, (3) không tà dâm, (4) không nói dối, (5) không uống các chất say, (6) không đeo đồ trang sức hoặc xức nước hoa, (7) không nghe ca hát hoặc xem khiêu vũ, (8) không ngủ trên giường cao hoặc giường rộng, (9) không ăn uống không đúng giờ, tức là buổi trưa, và (10) không sở hữu những vật có giá trị như vàng và bạc. Ngài vẫn đưa ra lời khuyên về một số vấn đề chính trị và khuyên vua Anh Tông "bỏ rượu và thường cúng dường, hỗ trợ Tăng đoàn.*"[122]

Thập giới là giáo lý căn bản của Phật giáo, là cơ sở cho đạo đức xã hội. Trúc Lâm có ý hướng xây dựng một xã hội dựa trên nền tảng đạo đức Phật giáo. Một vị vua trẻ ngồi trên ngai vàng ủng hộ Phật giáo, một vị Thượng Hoàng làm du tăng giữa quần chúng. Sự kiện này là duy nhất và chưa từng có. "*Trúc Lâm thật sự đã góp phần củng cố vương triều và chế độ bằng những hoạt động tín ngưỡng tích cực trong dân gian*".[123]

---

121. https://terebess.hu/zen/mesterek/Tran-Nhan-Tong.html

122. https://terebess.hu/zen/mesterek/Tran-Nhan-Tong.html

123. Việt Nam Phật giáo Sử luận (*History of Vietnamese Buddhism*), tập 1,2,3. Nguyễn Lang (aka Zen Master Thích Nhất Hạnh), Lá Bối. 1973,

Mùa đông năm ấy, 1304, vua Trần Anh Tông thỉnh Hòa thượng Hương Vân Đại Đầu Đà vào kinh thành truyền Bồ tát giới cho hàng nam nữ cư sĩ. Sau đó, Ngài đến trú tại chùa Sùng Nghiêm, núi Linh Sơn, thọ giới Bồ tát và dạy Thiền cho đại chúng.

Những vị vua thọ giới Bồ tát là những vị phát nguyện dùng khả năng và quyền lực của địa vị hoàng gia để phục vụ nhân dân dựa trên hạnh bồ tát. Ngày Trúc Lâm Thiền sư vào kinh thành, quần thần theo vua ra đón Trúc Lâm Quốc sư. Thấy vua Trần Anh Tông phát nguyện thọ bồ tát giới, họ cũng quy y Tam bảo (tuân theo Phật, pháp, tăng) và giữ Ngũ giới (không: sát sanh, trộm cắp, tà dâm,nói dối và say xỉn).

Về hình thức, cả một triều đình vua là thiên tử trở thành triều đình Phật giáo và một xã hội dựa trên Phật giáo với những công dân của họ sống một đời sống đạo đức như những vị vua thiền sư của họ.

5.7. Nhị Tổ Thiền Phái Trúc Lâm

Sơ tổ Trúc Lâm là tấm gương của một vị Tăng, một vị hoàng đế có tài và đức. Trong thời gian du hành nơi nhân gian, Trúc Lâm cũng có ý tìm một người kế thừa pháp

https://langmai.org/tang-kinh-cac/vien-sach/giang-kinh/viet-nam- phat-giao-su-luan/chuong-12-tran-nhan-tong-va-thien-phai-truc-lam/

học, tức là người có thể tiếp tục sự nghiệp hoằng pháp của mình tại nhân gian.

Năm 1304, khi Ngài đến làng Nam Sách, Trúc Lâm gặp một thanh niên hai mươi mốt tuổi muốn đi tu tên là Đồng Kiên Cương. Thấy dáng vẻ khác thường của vị này, Trúc Lâm tự nhủ: "Chàng trai này có tuệ nhãn, tương lai nhất định sẽ trở thành một vị pháp sư." Mừng vì sự gặp gỡ này, Trúc Lâm đặt tên cho chàng thanh niên là Thiện Lai, cho thọ giới Sa di và cho theo học với Hòa thượng Tính Giác. Thiện Lai sau này trở thành Pháp Loa, vị tổ thứ hai của Thiền phái Trúc Lâm.

"Pháp Loa chỉ làm sa di hơn một năm. Năm 1305, Trúc Lâm đã cho ông thọ đại giới làm Tỳ kheo và Bồ tát. Năm 1306, Ngài được bổ nhiệm làm giảng sư tại chùa Siêu Loại. Chính tổ thứ nhất đã dạy Pháp Loa từ các sách lịch sử Phật giáo như Truyền Đăng Lục I (Truyền đăng đăng lục) và Đại Tuệ Ngữ Lục."[124]

5.8. Đệ tử Tăng Ni thiền môn và Truyền Thừa Thiền Phái Trúc Lâm

Ngoài Pháp Loa, vị tổ thứ hai của Trúc Lâm thì Tổ Trúc Lâm còn có các đệ tử xuất gia khác như Ngài Bảo Sát, Bảo Phác, Pháp Không, Pháp Cổ và Huệ Nghiêm. Ngoài ra, theo biểu đồ của Huệ Nghiêm trong sách Tuệ Trung Thượng Sĩ Ngữ Lục, trong số các đệ tử của Trúc Lâm có Pháp Tràng, Hương Tràng, Hương Sơn và Mật Tạng.

5.9. Dòng Thiền Trúc Lâm

Thiền tông đã thăng trầm theo vận mệnh đất nước; tuy nhiên, theo sách *Văn hiến triều Lý-Trần (Thơ văn Lý Trần)*[125] thì Thiền phái Trúc Lâm có một danh sách dài

124. Ibid.

125. Thơ Văn Lý Trần. Nguyễn Huệ Chi. NXB Khoa Học Xã Hội. Hà

những người kế thừa và phát triển ngọn đèn Thiền trong thế kỷ XX và XXI như sau:

1. Thiền sư Trần Nhân Tông tức Hương Vân đại đầu đà (1258–1308)
2. Thiền sư Pháp Loa (1284¬1330)
3. Thiền sư Huyền Quang (1254–1334)
4. Thiền sư An Tâm
5. Thiền sư Phù Vân Tĩnh Lự
6. Thiền sư Vô Trước
7. Thiền sư Quốc Nhất
8. Thiền sư Viên Minh
9. Thiền sư Đạo Huệ
10. Thiền sư Viên Ngộ
11. Thiền sư Tổng Trì
12. Thiền sư Khuê Sâm
13. Thiền sư Sơn Đăng
14. Thiền sư Hương Sơn
15. Thiền sư Trí Dung
16. Thiền sư Huệ Quang
17. Thiền sư Chân Trụ
18. Thiền sư Vô Phiền
19. Thiền sư Thanh Từ (thế kỷ XX - XXI)...

5.10. Những Tác phẩm của Vua Trần Nhân Tông

Là vị thiền sư Trúc Lâm giác ngộ, còn là vị vua yêu nước, vua Trần Nhân Tông rất đau xót khi giặc ngoại xâm kéo đến đánh Đại Việt. Ông đã viết nhiều sắc dụ, văn tế,

Nội 1988. File PDF.

thơ văn bày tỏ nỗi lòng của mình đối với đất nước và Phật giáo. Các tác phẩm như:

- Thiền Lâm Thiết Chủy Ngữ Lục (Thiền ngữ)
- Tăng Già Toái Sự (Những Rắc Rối Hàng Ngày của Tu Sĩ)
- Thạch Thất My Ngữ (Nghịch Ngôn trong Nhà Thiền) của vua Trần Anh Tông chép vào Đại Tạng Kinh cho lưu hành.
- Đại Hương Hải Ấn Thi Tập (Tập thơ Dấu Ấn Biển Cả Hương Thơm Ngát)
- Trần Nhân Tông Thi Tập (Tập thơ của Trần Nhân Tông)
- Trung Hưng Thực Lục (2 tập) Ghi lại Cuộc Xâm Lăng của Quân Nguyên

Theo Nguyễn Huệ Chi, Trần Thị Băng Thanh, Đỗ Văn Hỷ và Trần Tú Châu, các biên tập viên của cuốn Văn Thơ thời Lý Trần (2 tập) cho biết rằng "*Thơ Trần Nhân Tông có tính chất kết hợp nhuần nhuyễn giữa triết lý và thế sự, giữa cảm thông, lạc quan, yêu đời, tấm lòng vị tha của một nhân cách lớn và những rung động tinh tế, yêu tự do của một nghệ sĩ.*"[126] Các câu thơ sau đây minh chứng cho điều đó:

Xã tắc hai phen chồn ngựa đá
Non sông nghìn thuở vững âu vàng.
(Toàn tập Trần Nhân Tông)[127]

Ở đời vui đạo hãy tùy duyên,

126. https://vietbooks.info/threads/tho-van-ly-tran-tap-2-quyen-thuong-nxb-khoa-hoc-xa-hoi-1988-nguyen- hue-chi-965-trang.1740/

127. https://zingnews.vn/9-cau-noi-luu-danh-muon-doi-cua-de-vuong-danh-than-nuoc-viet-post873836.html

Đói cứ ăn đi mệt ngủ liền.
Có báu trong nhà thôi tìm kiếm,
Vô Tâm Đối Cảnh Hỏi Chi Thiền
(Cư Trần Lạc Đạo Phú)[128]

Số đời một hơi thở
Lòng người hai biển vàng
Cung ma dồn quá lắm
Cõi Phật vui nào hơn.
(Trần Nhân Tông - Đức Vua Sáng Tổ Một Dòng Thiền)[129]

Tháp thờ Trần Nhân Tông ở Tháp Huế

128. Toàn tập Trần Nhân Tông (Whole set on Trần Nhân Tông) Lê Mạnh Thát (In lần thứ 3 có sửa chữa bổ sung). Viện Nghiên Cứu Phật Học Việt Nam. NXB Phương Đông. 1999

129. Trần Nhân Tông - Đức Vua Sáng Tổ Một Dòng Thiền (Trần Nhân Tông, The King Who Founded A Zen School). Translated and Commented by Nguyen Giac;.
https://thuvienhoasen.org/a11751/tran-nhan-tong

Cảnh vắng sống yên tự tại hồn,
Bóng tùng gió mát thổi từng cơn.
Dưới gốc, giường thiền, kinh một quyển,
Thanh nhàn hai chữ; đáng muôn đồng.
(Trần Nhân Tông - Đức Vua Sáng Tổ Một Dòng Thiền)[130]

Vua Trần Nhân Tông còn là nhà thơ tiêu biểu của thời Trần. Thơ Ngài có sức hấp dẫn đặc biệt, không chỉ bởi những ý tưởng cao cả, sâu sắc mà còn bởi vẻ đẹp đạt tới sự tinh tế của ngôn từ và cách diễn đạt. Ngài được xem như nhà thơ, nhà văn hóa, tiêu biểu của nước Đại Việt thời trung đại. Tên "Trần Nhân Tông" và "Trúc Lâm Thiền Sư" đã được đặt cho nhiều thiền viện, chùa tự, trường học, hội quán, đường phố, tỉnh thành trên đất nước Việt Nam để tưởng nhớ vị Thiền sư từ bi và kiệt xuất.

Bộ phim "Phật Hoàng Trần Nhân Tông" do Tổng đạo diễn, NSƯT Văn Lượng và các cộng sự của Hãng phim

130. Trần Nhân Tông - Đức Vua Sáng Tổ Một Dòng Thiền (Trần Nhân Tông, The King Who Founded A Zen School). Translated and Commented by Nguyen Giac.
https://thuvienhoasen.org/a11751/tran-nhan-tong

Truyền hình Hải Phòng (HFS) đã bắt đầu tiến trình sản xuất bộ phim sử thi dài 45 tập này.

Với tâm huyết của các đơn vị sản xuất và sự đóng góp của các nhà nghiên cứu Phật giáo, văn hóa, lịch sử, hy vọng rằng bộ phim Phật HoàngTrần Nhân Tông sẽ là "*Một tác phẩm nghệ thuật xứng tầm với tầm vóc của một nhân vật lỗi lạc trong lịch sử dân tộc và thế giới.*"[131]

5.11. Tổ sư Trúc Lâm viên tịch và di sản để lại

Năm 1307, khi Ngài Pháp Loa mới hai mươi bốn tuổi, Ngài Trúc Lâm đã viết bài kệ, truyền y bát truyền cho Pháp Loa. Ngày mồng một Tết Nguyên Đán (1308), Đại Sư Trúc Lâm viên tịch. Ngài Trúc Lâm chính thức bổ nhiệm Pháp Loa kế vị trụ trì chùa Siêu Loại, vị tổ thứ hai của thiền phái Trúc Lâm. Sự kiện này được thực hiện dưới sự chứng minh của Vua Trần Anh Tông.

Thiền Sử thuật lại giây phút Thiền sư Trúc Lâm cảm thấy tự tại nhập định viên tịch như sau:

"Ngày mười tám tháng ấy, thiền sư Trúc Lâm đi bộ đến chùa Từ Lâm núi An Kỳ Sanh. Cảm thấy nhức đầu, Ngài nói với hai nhà sư trong chùa: "Tôi muốn leo lên đỉnh Ngọa Vân, nhưng chân tôi yếu. Tôi nên làm gì đây?"

Hai nhà sư trả lời rằng họ sẽ giúp khiêng Ngài ấy lên. Đến chùa Ngọa Vân trên đỉnh núi, Ngài nói lời cảm ơn với hai nhà sư và giục: "Hãy xuống núi lo Phật sự đi; đừng xem nhẹ vấn đề sinh tử."

Ngày mười chín tháng đó, Ngài sai thị giả Pháp Không đến chùa Từ Tiêu, núi Yên Tử, bảo Ngài Bảo Sát xuống gặp gấp. Ngày hai mươi mốt, Bảo Sát đến chùa Ngọa Vân. Thiền sư Trúc Lâm thấy vậy nói: "Ta đi đây. Tại sao ông đến muộn như vậy? Nếu ông vẫn chưa rõ về giáo lý nhà

131. https://nhandan.vn/bo-phim-su-thi-phat-hoang-tran-nhan-tong-post387865.html

Phật, hãy hỏi tôi ngay lúc này."

Bảo Sát nói: "Khi Mã Tổ cảm bệnh, sư trưởng hỏi: 'Thưa thầy, dạo này thầy cảm thấy thế nào?' Mã Tổ đáp:

'Nhật Diện Phật, Nguyệt Diện Phật', nghĩa là thế nào? Sư Trúc Lâm lớn tiếng nói: "Tam Hoàng Ngũ Đế, là cái gì?"

(Ở đây cần lưu ý. Nhật Diện Phật và Nguyệt Diện Phật là tên của hai vị Phật có khuôn mặt giống như mặt trời và mặt trăng, tương ứng. Cả hai tên đều được liệt kê trong Kinh Vạn Phật. Cuộc đời của Đức Phật Nhật Diện kéo dài 1.800 năm trong khi cuộc đời của Đức Phật Nguyệt Diện chỉ có một ngày một đêm.)

Bảo Sát lại hỏi: "Thế nào là câu cổ ngữ 'Hoa nở gấm gấm; phương nam trúc mọc, phương bắc cây mọc' nghĩa là gì? Thiền sư Trúc Lâm đáp: "Họ đã làm cho ông bị mù."

Bảo Sát ngừng hỏi. Sau đó, bầu trời tối tăm và ảm đạm trong vài ngày. Chim và khỉ trong rừng kêu khóc thảm thiết. Vào đêm ngày mồng một tháng mười một năm ấy, bầu trời trở nên quang đãng và đầy sao lấp lánh. Tổ Trúc Lâm hỏi Bảo Sát: "Bây giờ là mấy giờ?"

Bảo Sát đáp: "Giờ tý".

Thiền sư Trúc Lâm vén rèm nhìn ra ngoài nói: "Đã đến lúc ta phải đi rồi".

Bảo Sát hỏi: "Ngài định đi đâu?"

Thiền sư Trúc Lâm đọc bài thơ này:

Tất cả pháp chẳng sinh
Tất cả pháp chẳng diệt.
Nếu hay hiểu như thế
Chư Phật thường hiện tiền
Nào có đến đi gì.
(Nhất thiết pháp bất sinh

Nhất thiết pháp bất diệt
Nhược năng như thị giải
Chư Phật thường hiện tiền
Hà khứ lai chi hữu dã).

Bảo Sát hỏi:

- Chỉ như khi chẳng sinh chẳng diệt là thế nào?

Ngài liền nhằm ngay miệng Bảo Sát tát cho một cái, bảo:

- Chớ nói mớ.

Nói xong, Ngài nằm nghiêng bên phải như sư tử, lặng lẽ mà tịch."

Đây là những phút cuối cùng của một nhân vật cao quý và vương giả đã cống hiến cuộc đời mình cho sự nghiệp của giáo pháp, đất nước và dân tộc. Sau mười lăm năm trị vì, Trần Nhân Tông nằm xuống như một con sư tử, an nhiên thị tịch ở tuổi 51 vào năm 1308. Tổ Trúc Lâm chỉ sống được nửa thế kỷ; tuy nhiên, Thiền phái Trúc Lâm do Ngài sáng lập ngày nay đã trở thành thiền phái lớn nhất Việt Nam, đặc biệt với sự hỗ trợ của Đại Thiền sư Thích Thanh Từ của thế kỷ XX và XXI.

Trần Nhân Tông nằm nghiêng bên phải

như Đức Phật nhập Niết Bàn

Khi Trần Nhân Tông thăng hà, triều đình và nhân dân thương tiếc vang dội khắp cả nước. Một nhà sử học nhận xét: *"Hiếm có vị vua nào trong quốc sử được ghi lại đầy đủ về sự ngưỡng mộ của nhân dân sau khi thăng hà..."*[132]

"Ngài Pháp Loa tuân theo ý thầy, làm lễ hỏa táng và thu thập các mảnh xá lợi xương ngũ sắc. Vua Trần Anh Tông cho xây bảo tháp trong sân chùa Vàm Yên trên núi Yên Tử. Vua đặt tên cho tháp là "Đại Thánh Trần Triều Trúc Lâm Đầu Đà Tĩnh Tuệ Giác Hoàng Điều Ngự Tổ Phật."[133]

132. https://nhandan.vn/bo-phim-su-thi-phat-hoang-tran-nhan-tong-post387865.html

133. Lê Văn Hưu, Phan Phu Tiên, Ngô Sĩ Liên. 1993. 193.

Một phần Xá lợi của Trần Nhân Tông được thờ tại Bảo tháp Huệ Quang

Tượng Phật Giác Hoàng Trần Nhân Tông tại Bảo tháp Huệ Quang

VI. SO SÁNH SỰ VĨ ĐẠI GIỮA HOÀNG ĐẾ A-DỤC VÀ VUA TRẦN NHÂN TÔNG

Giống như Đại đế A-dục, vua Trần Nhân Tông đã đi khắp mọi miền đất nước để khuyến khích người dân sống một cuộc sống tâm linh, vâng giữ mười điều thiện (thập thiện) để đời sống phát triển tốt hơn.

Cả hai vị vua đều có nhiều điểm tương đồng như sau:

"*Cả hai vị hoàng đế đều thuộc các triều đại hùng mạnh của Ấn Độ và Việt Nam—Ashoka Đại đế của triều đại Maurya và Hoàng đế Trần Nhân Tông của triều đại nhà Trần.*"[134]

Thời kỳ trị vì của Vua Pháp A-dục là thời kỳ huy hoàng của Phật giáo ở Ấn Độ, và ở Việt Nam cũng vậy dưới thời trị vì của vua Trần Nhân Tông.

"*Khi chúng ta đi qua những câu chuyện về cuộc đời của cả Đại đế A-dục và Vua Trần Nhân Tông, chúng ta thấy cả hai đều có tình thương bao la đối với nhân loại cũng như đối với Phật giáo, bất kể lĩnh vực hay vấn đề nào.*"[135]

Hoàng đế Ashoka tiến hành chiến tranh để mở rộng vương quốc của mình và tạo ra chủ quyền độc lập tối cao. Vua Trần Nhân Tông đã tiến hành chiến tranh để bảo vệ đất nước, công dân và nền văn hóa của mình khỏi quân xâm lược Mông Cổ.

Tuy nhiên, cả hai đều đã tận mắt chứng kiến cảnh đổ máu và rút ra bài học về giới sát sanh. Theo các nhà sử học, hàng triệu người đã chết vì những cuộc chiến đó trong khi tài sản ở một số khu vực bị phá hủy hoàn toàn. Cả hai vị vua đều cống hiến quyền lực hoàng gia của mình để truyền bá đạo Phật thực hiện các hoạt động có lợi cho Đại Tăng đoàn và các thần dân thân yêu của họ.

134. Lê Văn Hưu, Phan Phu Tiên, Ngô Sĩ Liên. 1993. 192

135. Ibid

Tương truyền rằng vua Trần Nhân Tông không ăn thịt cá. Hoàng đế A-dục, về vấn đề này, tiến xa hơn, là đã cấm giết mổ động vật trên toàn quốc. Mặt khác, theo cách sống, cả hai đều dũng cảm và có đủ can đảm để đối mặt và xử lý mọi tình huống cũng như làm việc không mệt mõi để phục vụ người dân cho tốt đời đẹp đạo. Cả hai đều làm việc không giới hạn để phục vụ người dân vì cuộc sống tốt đẹp hơn.

Có vẻ như cả hai có thể đã phải đối mặt với những thách thức khi họ truyền bá Phật giáo, vì có những người khác theo những tín ngưỡng truyền thống khác nhau. Khi Hoàng đế A-dục đưa Phật giáo trở thành tôn giáo phổ biến ở thế giới và Hoàng đế Trần Nhân Tông đã đưa Thiền phái Trúc Lâm trở nên mạnh mẽ trong đế chế của mình, phổ toàn lãnh thổ Việt nam, và những đất nước mà cư dân Việt nam sinh sống và xuyên suốt cho đến thế kỷ XXI.

VII. ĐÓNG GÓP LỚN CHO HÒA BÌNH THẾ GIỚI VÀ HẠNH PHÚC XÃ HỘI

Hoàng đế A-dục của Ấn Độ và Hoàng đế Trần Nhân Tông của Việt Nam đều có những đóng góp to lớn cho hòa bình thế giới và sự hòa hợp xã hội cho đất nước và nhân dân của họ.

Từ một vị vua giết người hung tàn, Đại đế A-dục đã thức tỉnh khi nhìn thấy dòng sông đẫm máu từ cuộc chinh phục Kalinga ở bờ biển phía Đông. Từ đó, ông đã trở thành một đệ tử chân chính, nhân hậu của Đức Phật, chủ trương từ bi, trí tuệ và đặc biệt là bất bạo động, không làm tổn thương thân xác và tinh thần của người khác.

Nhìn vào lịch sử Phật giáo là nhìn vào lịch sử của lòng vị tha, hy sinh, lo cho mọi người dân, giúp họ vượt qua khổ đau, sống an lạc, hạnh phúc trong hiện tại và tương lai. Vì vậy, nhà vua A-dục đã dùng pháp của Đức Thế Tôn để trị nước như sau:

7.1. Mười giới

1) Không sát sinh hoặc khuyến khích người khác sát sinh.
2) Không ăn cắp hoặc khuyến khích người khác ăn cắp.
3) Không tham gia vào các hành vi dâm ô hoặc khuyến khích người khác làm như vậy.
4) Không được dùng lời dối trá hoặc khuyến khích người khác làm như vậy.
5) Không trao đổi, bán đồ uống có cồn hoặc khuyến khích người khác làm như vậy.
6) Không loan truyền những việc làm sai trái của đại chúng Tăng ni, Phật tử, không khuyến khích những người khác làm như vậy.
7) Không tự khen mình, nói xấu người khác hoặc khuyến khích người khác làm như vậy.
8) Không keo kiệt hoặc khuyến khích người khác làm như vậy.
9) Không nuôi lòng tức giận hoặc khuyến khích người khác tức giận.
10) Không nói xấu Phật, Pháp, Tăng (Tam Bảo) hoặc khuyến khích người khác làm như vậy.

Giữ giới để tránh nhân quả xấu, tăng trưởng việc thiện, tạo môi trường an vui, hạnh phúc cho mình, gia đình và cộng đồng.

7.2. Sáu điều hòa hợp (Lục hòa)

1) Hòa hợp khi có cùng quan điểm
2) Hòa đồng giữ giới
3) Hòa thuận chung sống
4) Hòa hợp trong lời nói không mâu thuẫn

5) Hòa hợp trong việc trải nghiệm pháp lạc

6) Hòa hợp trong việc chia sẻ lợi ích.

Sáu cách hòa hợp giúp kết nối các cá nhân như một tổng thể, những người có thể cùng sống, cùng làm việc, cùng chia sẻ và cùng tiến bộ trên con đường tâm linh. Đất nước giàu mạnh là nhờ sự hòa hợp của mỗi người, mỗi gia đình và cộng đồng. Mười Giới và Sáu Hòa Hợp là một sức mạnh lớn cho hòa bình thế giới và hòa hợp xã hội.

Vua A-dục đã cho khắc những lời dạy này trên các cột đá như một sắc lệnh duy trì sự hòa hợp và hòa bình. Ngài ra lệnh cho các phái đoàn Phật giáo mang thông điệp hạnh phúc và giải thoát này ra ngoài biên giới Ấn Độ đến Tích Lan, Thái Lan, Lào, Trung Quốc, Việt Nam, v.v. Cụ thể như nhà vua đã gửi con trai của mình, thái tử, tức Tỳ kheo Mahinda (Mahendra), đến Tích Lan để thành lập Phật giáo, và sau đó, đã gửi con gái của mình, Công chúa tức Tỳ-kheo-ni Sanghamitra, sang Tích Lan để thành lập Ni đoàn, giúp nữ giới xuất gia tu học.

Ngoài ra, Đại đế A-dục còn là một nhà hảo tâm đã hỗ trợ tăng đoàn rất lớn bằng cách thường xuyên hỗ trợ tịnh tài và tứ vật dụng (tịnh xá, thuốc men, y áo và thực phẩm). Để giữ cho tăng đoàn chuyên tâm tu tập thanh tịnh, bất kỳ nhà sư nào giả vờ thâm nhập vào tăng đoàn mà không thật tu tập sẽ bị trừng phạt nghiêm khắc. Đại đế A-dục đã đóng vai trò là mạnh thường quân đắc lực củng cố Phật giáo. Nhà vua cũng cho xây dựng nhiều chùa tháp ở nhiều bang của Ấn Độ cổ đại. Ngày nay, các nhà khảo cổ học đã đang khám phá các công trình cống hiến của Đại đế A-dục.

Đại đế A-dục là vị vua đầu tiên được cho là đã truyền bá thông điệp bất bạo động, từ bi và trí tuệ của Đức Phật ra khỏi Ấn Độ. Đạo Phật là cách sống an lạc, hạnh phúc, chánh niệm và tỉnh thức. Phương pháp nầy có thể cũng cố việc chuyển đổi xã hội thành một nơi có trật tự, an toàn, công bằng, hòa bình và hạnh phúc. Phương pháp này đã được chấp nhận, tồn tại và hòa nhập ở nhiều quốc gia không phân biệt nguồn gốc quốc gia, tình trạng hôn nhân, dân tộc, màu da, giới tính, chủng tộc, tuổi tác và nghề nghiệp. Phật giáo có thể hòa hợp một cách uyển chuyển với các nền văn hóa, tôn giáo, triết học và tổ chức khác để cùng củng cố một thế giới với sự giải thoát, xứng đáng để sống an bình.

Cũng như với Hoàng đế A-dục, vua Trần Nhân Tông lấy Thập giới, Lục hòa và nghiên cứu triết lý Thiền của Phật giáo làm tư tưởng chủ đạo để xây dựng xã hội dựa trên Phật giáo. Ngài lãnh đạo nhân dân và đệ tử Phật giáo trau giồi trí đức, đoàn kết lòng dân, bảo vệ đất nước khỏi giặc ngoại xâm, xây dựng đất nước thái bình.

Khi đất nước bị giặc ngoại xâm, vua Trần Nhân Tông gác lại việc tu hành để bảo vệ đất nước. Ngài trị quốc, yên dân, thể hiện tinh thần tự cường dân tộc, được nhân dân đời đời ghi nhớ.

Khi đất nước hòa bình, Ngài chú trọng đến giáo dục, chọn lọc quan trường, xây dựng bộ máy nhà nước liêm chính, để xã hội công bằng, bình đẳng và phát triển.

Khi thái tử đủ trưởng thành để điều hành vương quốc, Ngài đã nhường ngôi cho con và trở thành một nhà sư sống cuộc đời giản dị, khổ hạnh để tìm kiếm chân lý trên một ngọn núi xa xôi. Ngài đã giác ngộ và chia sẻ con đường giác ngộ (Thiền Trúc Lâm) cho tất cả mọi người, được minh họa rõ ràng qua các bài thơ, sắc lệnh và tác phẩm của Ngài vào thời nhà Trần.

Với trí tuệ và tầm nhìn sâu xa của một vị Thiền sư, Ngài hiểu rằng giáo lý nhà Phật là nơi cứu khổ cứu nạn, giúp chúng sinh bỏ ác làm lành, sống thanh tịnh. Làm vua phải có đạo đức vì chúng sinh, Thiền sư Trúc Lâm đã xây dựng một mô hình tốt để mang lại sự hòa hợp cho Tăng đoàn, hoàng gia và xã hội cho người dân và chúng đệ tử Phật giáo của mình.

Ngài đã áp dụng thực hành sáu pháp Hòa hợp của Phật giáo để xây dựng một nước Đại Việt thái bình thịnh trị.

Thứ nhất, về mặt ngoại giao, Vua Trần Nhân Tông đã nỗ lực xây dựng tình hữu nghị thân thiết với nước láng giềng nằm ở biên giới phía Nam là Champa. Để thắt chặt mối quan hệ ngoại giao đang có đà tốt đẹp, để ngăn cản người Đại Việt cướp bóc các nước láng giềng Champa và tăng cường gìn giữ hòa bình, vua Trần Nhân Tông đã cử con gái là Công chúa Huyền Trân sang Champa để kết hôn với Vua Chế Mân. "*Về việc hứa hôn kén rể, vua Chế Mân đã dâng hai châu Châu Ô và Châu Lý (nay là Thuận Châu và Hóa Châu của Việt Nam*)."[136] Hiện tại hai châu này là quận Thuận Hoá thuộc thành phố Huế. Kể từ đó, cả hai nước đã kết bạn với nhau về một mối, sự hòa bình và hòa hợp này mở rộng đến các khu vực xung quanh.

Thứ hai, để củng cố nền hòa bình lâu dài, Vua Trần Nhân Tông đã thả các tù binh Mông-Nguyên mà quân đội bắt được trong ba cuộc chiến tranh để tạo điều kiện thuận lợi cho quan hệ hòa bình giữa hai nước, một quyết định sáng suốt và mềm dẻo trong chính sách đối ngoại của Đại Việt lúc bấy giờ. Có lẽ, vì thế mà Trần Nhân Tông được thế giới coi là người tiêu biểu nhất cho tinh thần hòa giải xã hội và hòa bình thế giới.

VIII. KẾT LUẬN

Trong lịch sử dân tộc và Phật giáo, Đại đế A-dục và Vua Trần Nhân Tông là những vị hoàng đế kiệt xuất của Ấn Độ và Việt Nam. Các Ngài chủ trương đưa đạo Phật nhập thế, tích cực truyền bá trong nhân dân, phát huy tinh thần hòa hợp trăm họ, xây dựng vun đắp nền độc lập, tự cường, nhân dân hòa hợp, vua cùng thần hòa hợp, phụ tử hòa hợp, hòa thuận giữa vợ chồng, gia đình và quốc gia. Tư tưởng đó là nguồn gốc sức mạnh trường tồn của dân tộc theo thời gian đã trở thành truyền thống của dân tộc. Họ đã tạo ra một xã hội văn minh và tốt đẹp dựa trên nền tảng Phật giáo cho chính họ và cộng đồng toàn cầu. Thật

136. https://sdl.thuathienhue.gov.vn/?g=20&cn=1&id=232&tc=4165

vậy, Hoàng đế A-dục và Vua Trần Nhân Tông là những người gìn giữ hòa bình thế giới và sự hòa hợp cho xã hội "*chỉ có sự chiến thắng của Đạo Pháp mới thực là một cuộc chiến thắng vô thượng; ai ai cũng nhờ cuộc chiến thắng ấy mà được an cư lạc nghiệp.*" (Hoàng đế A-dục)[137]

Cuộc đời của cả hai vị hoàng đế đều là một di sản vô giá cho hậu thế. Các Ngài đã trở thành những nhân vật thế giới, là nguồn cảm hứng cho các thế hệ tương lai.

Kolkata, ngày 02 tháng 07 năm 2023

Ni Sư Tiến sĩ T.N. Giới Hương

huongsentemple@gmail.com

Fy giới thiệu diễn giả Ni sư Tiến sĩ T.N. Giới Hương

137. Thích Nguyên Tạng. Một ông vua hộ trì phật pháp. 09/09/2015. https://thuvienhoasen.org/a23735/dai-de-a-duc-mot-ong-vua-ho-tri-phat-phap

Hình lưu niệm trước cổng Siddharth United Social Welfare Mission, Chinar Park, Kolkata, Tây Bengal

Những Diễn Giả Phật Giáo

Toàn cảnh của buổi hội thảo Buddha Priya Mahathero

Các diễn giả thuyết trình

Sư cô T.N.. Trí Minh (em gái của Ns Giới Hương) thuyết trình

Từ trái sang: Ni sư Tiến sĩ T.N. Giới Hương, Sư cô Trí Minh và các Sư cô đệ tử Sc Viên Bảo, Sc Viên Nhuận và Sc Đức Trí

NGUỒN THAM KHẢO

- Aher, D.C. Ashoka the Great. Delhi, India: B.R. Publishing Corporation, 1995.
- Ayyar, Sulochana. Costumes and Ornaments as Depicted in the Early Sculptures of Gwarlior Museum. Delhi, India: Mittal Publications, South Asia Books, 1987.
- Bandarkar, B.R. Ashoka. Kolkata, India: Calcutta University, 1999.
- Bapat, Professor P.V. ed. 2500 Years of Buddhism. India: Department of Information, Government of India, 1959.
- Bhandarakar, D.R. Aśoka. Calcutta, India: Calcutta University Press, 1969.
- H.G. Wells (1866–1946). A Short History of the World. 1922.
- Bongard-Levin, G.M. Mauryan India. New Delhi, India: Sterling Publishers, 1985
- Chand, S. Kalinga Rock Edicts–Ancient India. New Delhi, India: S. Chand and Co. Ltd. Publishers, 2008.
- Chauhan, Giand Chand. Origin and Growth of Feudalism in Early India: From the Mauryas to AD 650. Delhi, India: Munshiram Manoharlal Publishers, 2004.
- Đại Việt Sử Ký Toàn Thư (National Bureau for Historical Record). Lê Văn Hưu, Phan Phu Tiên, Ngô Sĩ Liên. Viện Khoa Học Xã Hội Việt Nam dịch (1985–1992).

  https://www.tuvienquangduc.com.au/lichsu/lichsuVietnam/Daivietsukytoanthu.pdf

- Dharmapala, Ven. Maha Thera. Ashoka. Kolkata, India: The Bengal Buddhist Association, 1997.
- Gokhale, Balkrishna Govind. Ashoka Maurya. New York: Twayne Publishers, Inc., 1966.
- Thích Tâm Minh (2004) A Dục Vương, cuộc đời và sự nghiệp, NBX Tôn Giáo, VN
- Thích Nguyên Tạng. Một ông vua hộ trì Phật pháp. 09/09/2015.

  https://thuvienhoasen.org/a23735/dai-de-a-duc-mot- ong-vua-ho-tri-phat-phap
- Ven. Thích Nhất Hạnh, Việt Nam Phật giáo Sử luận (History of Vietnamese Buddhism), tập 1,2,3. Nguyễn Lang, Lá Bối. 1973.

  https://langmai.org/tang-kinh-cac/vien-sach/giang- kinh/viet-nam-phat-giao-su-luan/chuong-12-tran- nhan-tong-va-thien-phai-truc-lam/
- Hazra, Kanai Lal. Royal Patronage of Buddhism in Ancient India. New Delhi, India: D.K. Publications, 1984.
- Kiskalar, D.B. "Literary Value of Inscriptions of Ashoka," Journal of Indian History. New Delhi. Mahajan, V.D. Ancient India. New Delhi: S. Chand Publishing, 2016.
- Malasekera, Dr. G.P. ed. Encyclopaedia of Buddhism, Vol. II. Sri Lanka: Government of Ceylon, Colombo, 1967.
- Medhankara, Ven. Dr. Maha Thero. The Great Buddhist Emperors of Asia. Maharashrata, India: Bhoomi Prakashan. Nagpur, 1959.
- Nikam, N.A. and McKeon, Richard, eds. The Edicts of Ashoka. Chicago: University of Chicago Press, 1978.
- Smith, Vincent A. Aśoka and the Buddhist Emperors

of India. Delhi: Low Price Publications, 1930.

- Thích Hạnh Thành. Biên Niên Sử Thiền Tông Việt Nam (1010–2000).
- Toàn tập Trần Nhân Tông (Whole Set on Trần Nhân Tông) Lê Mạnh Thát, Third Edition. Viện Nghiên Cứu Phật Học Việt Nam. NXB Phương Đông. 1999.
- Trần Nhân Tông - Đức Vua Sáng Tổ Một Dòng Thiền (Trần Nhân Tông, The King Who Founded a Zen School). Translation and commentary by Nguyen Giac.

  https://thuvienhoasen.org/a11751/tran-nhan-tong-duc-vua-sang-to-mot-dong-thien-nguyen-giac
- Thích Thanh Từ. Vietnamese Zen in the Late Twentieth Century.

  https://thientruclam.info/ht-thich-thanh-tu/thien-tong-viet-nam-cuoi-the-ky-20. NXB Hồng Đức. 2016.

  https://hoavouu.com/a48178/bien-nien-su-thien-tong- viet-nam-1010-2000
- Thơ Văn Lý Trần. Nguyễn Huệ Chi. NXB Khoa Học Xã Hội. Hà Nội 1988.
- Thiền Uyển Tập Anh. Dịch giả Nguyễn Huệ Chi. Phân viện Nghiên cứu Phật Học.NXB Văn Học. Hà Nội 1990.

  http://thuongchieu.net/index.php/phapthoai/suong/1960-pht-giao-thin-tong-vit-nam

BAO ANH LAC BOOKSHELF

Dr. Bhikṣuṇī TN Giới Hương composed

1.1. THE VIETNAMESE BOOKS

1. *Bồ-tát và Tánh Không Trong Kinh Tạng Pali và* Đại *Thừa* (Boddhisattva and Sunyata in the Early and Developed Buddhist Traditions).
2. *Ban Mai Xứ Ấn* (The Dawn in India) - *Tuyển tập các Tiểu Luận Phật Giáo* (Collection of Buddhist Essays), (3 tập).
3. *Sārnātha - Vườn Nai – Chiếc Nôi Phật Giáo* (Sārnātha - Deer Park–The Cradle of Buddhism).
4. *Quy Y Tam Bảo và Năm Giới* (Take Refuge in Three Gems and Keep the Five Precepts).
5. *Vòng Luân Hồi* (The Cycle of Life).
6. *Hoa Tuyết Milwaukee* (Snowflake in Milwaukee).
7. *Luân Hồi trong Lăng Kính Lăng Nghiêm* (The Rebirth in Śūrangama Sūtra).
8. *Nghi Thức Hộ Niệm, Cầu Siêu* (The Ritual for the Deceased).
9. *Quan* Âm *Quảng Trần* (The Commentary of Avalokiteśvara Bodhisattva).
10. *Nữ Tu và Tù Nhân Hoa Kỳ* (A Nun and American

Inmates).

11. *Nếp Sống Tỉnh Thức của Đức Đạt Lai Lạt Ma Thứ XIV* (The Awakened Mind of the 14th Dalai Lama).

12. *A-Hàm: Mưa pháp chuyển hóa phiền não* (*Agama – A Dharma Rain transforms the Defilement*), 2 tập.

13. *Góp Từng Hạt Nắng Perris* (Collection of Sunlight in Perris).

14. *Pháp Ngữ của Kinh Kim Cang* (The Key Words of Vajracchedikā-Prajñāpāramitā-Sūtra).

15. *Tập Thơ Nhạc Nắng Lăng Nghiêm* (Songs and Poems of Śūraṅgama Sunlight).

16. *Nét Bút Bên Song Cửa* (Reflections at the Temple Window).

17. *Máy Nghe MP3 Hương Sen* (Hương Sen Digital Mp3 Radio Speaker): Các Bài Giảng, Sách, Bài viết và Thơ Nhạc của Thích Nữ Giới Hương (383/201 bài).

18. *DVD Giới Thiệu về Chùa* Hương Sen, USA (Introduction on Huong Sen Temple).

19. *Ni Giới Việt Nam Hoằng Pháp tại Hoa Kỳ* (Sharing the Dharma - Vietnamese Buddhist Nuns in the United States).

20. *Tuyển Tập 40 Năm Tu Học & Hoằng Pháp của Ni sư Giới* Hương (Forty Years in the Dharma: A Life of Study and Service—Venerable Bhikkhuni Giới Hương), Thích Nữ Viên Quang, TN Viên Nhuận, TN Viên Tiến, and TN Viên Khuông.

21. *Tập Thơ Nhạc Lối Về Sen Nở* (*Songs and Poems of Lotus Blooming on the Way*).

22. *Nghi Thức* Công Phu *Khuya – Thần Chú Thủ Lăng Nghiêm* (Śūraṅgama Mantra).
23. *Nghi Thức Cầu An – Kinh Phổ* Môn (The Universal Door Sūtra).
24. *Nghi Thức Cầu An – Kinh Dược Sư* (The Medicine Buddha Sūtra).
25. *Nghi Thức Sám Hối Hồng Danh* (The Sūtra of Confession at many Buddha Titles).
26. *Nghi Thức* Công Phu *Chiều – Mông* Sơn *Thí Thực* (The Ritual Donating Food to Hungry Ghosts).
27. *Khóa Tịnh* Độ *– Kinh A Di* Đà (The Amitabha Buddha Sūtra).
28. *Nghi Thức Cúng Linh và Cầu Siêu* (The Rite for Deceased and Funeral Home).
29. *Nghi Lễ Hàng Ngày - 50 Kinh Tụng và các Lễ* Vía *trong Năm* (The Daily Chanting Rituals and Annual Ceremonies).
30. *Hương* Đạo *Trong* Đời *2022* (Tuyển tập 60 Bài Thi trong Cuộc Thi Viết Văn Ứng Dụng Phật Pháp 2022 - A Collection of Writings on the Practicing of Buddhism in Daily Life in the Writing Contest 2022).
31. *Hương Pháp 2022* (Tuyển Tập Các Bài Thi Trúng Giải Cuộc Thi Viết Văn Ứng Dụng Phật Pháp 2022 - A Collection of the Winning Writings on the Practicing of Buddhism in Daily Life in the Writing Contest 2022).
32. *Giới* Hương - *Thơm Ngược Gió Ngàn* (Giới Hương – The Virtue Fragrance Against the Thousand Winds), Nguyên Hà.

33. *Pháp Ngữ Kinh Hoa Nghiêm* (Buddha-avatamsaka-nāma-mahāvaipulya-sūtra) (2 tập).
34. *Tinh Hoa Kinh Hoa Nghiêm (The Core of Buddha-avatamsaka-nāma-mahāvaipulya-sūtra*).
35. *Phật Giáo – Tầm Nhìn Lịch Sử Và Thực Hành* (*Buddhism: A Historical and Practical Vision*). Hiệu đính: Thích Hạnh Chánh và Thích Nữ Giới Hương.
36. *Nhật ký Hành Thiền Vipassana và Kinh Tứ Niệm Xứ* (Diary: Practicing Vipassana and the Four Foundations of Mindfulness Sutta).
37. *Nghi cúng Giao Thừa* (New Year's Eve Ceremony).
38. *Nghi cúng Rằm Tháng Giêng* (the Ceremony of the First Month's Full Moon).
39. *Nghi thức Lễ Phật* Đản (The Buddha Birthday's Ceremony).
40. *Nghi thức Vu Lan* (The Ullambana Festival or Parent Day).
41. *Lễ* Vía Quan Âm *(*The Avolokiteshvara Day).
42. *Nghi cúng Thánh Tổ Kiều* Đàm *Di* (The Death Anniversary of Mahapajapati Gotami).
43. *Nghi thức cúng Tổ và Giác linh Sư trưởng* (The Ancestor Day).
44. *Nghi Lễ Chẩn Tế Mười Hai Loại Cô Hồn* (Offering Food to the Twelve Ghosts).
45. *Kỷ Yếu Lễ Tưởng Niệm Thánh Tổ Kiều* Đàm *Di tại Chùa* Hương Sen *năm 2024* (The Yearbook of the Commemoration of Mahapajapati Gotami at Huong Sen Temple in 2024).

46. *Nghi Thức Cầu Siêu Chư* Hương Linh Thai Nhi (Pray for the Abortion, Unborn Baby).

47. *Kim Quang Minh Kinh Sám Trai Thiên Khóa Nghi* (The Golden Light Sutra - Heavenly Course).

48. *Phật Giáo và Thánh Tích Sri Lanka* (Buddhism and Holy Buddhist Places in Sri Lanka).

49. Đấu Tranh Bất Bạo Động Là Nền Tảng Xây Dựng Hòa Bình Toàn Cầu (Nonviolent Struggle - The Foundation for Building Global Peace)

50. *Vũ Trụ Luận dưới lăng kính Khoa học và Phật Giáo* (Cosmology under the Lens of Science and Buddhism)

51. *COVID-19: Vai trò Phật Giáo trong Việc Chữa Lành* (COVID-19: The Role of Buddhism in Healing)

52. *Đại Dịch Coronavirus trong Thế Kỷ XXI* (Coronavirus Pandemic in the 21st Century)

53. *Đóng góp của Phật Giáo cho Hòa Bình Thế Giới và Hòa Hợp Xã Hội* (Contribution of Buddhism For World Peace & Social Harmony).

54. *Phật Giáo Toàn Cầu - Đặc Biệt Liên Kết Với Sri Lanka* (Global Spread of Buddhism with Special Reference to Sri Lanka).

55. *Phật Giáo Sri Lanka từ Thế Kỷ 19-21* (Buddhism In Sri Lanka during the Period of 19th to 21st Centuries)

56. *Ngày Nhà Giáo Việt Nam 20/11 – Tri Ân Người Khai Trí* (Vietnamese Teachers' Day November 20 - Gratitude to the Master guiding the knowledge)

57. *Lịch Sử Giáo Dục Phật Giáo và Các Học Viện Hiện Tại của Bhikkhu, bhikkhuni và Sīla Mātā tại Sri Lanka* (History of Buddhist Education and Current Institutes

of Bhikkhu, Bhikkhuni and Sīla Mātā in Sri Lanka)

1.2. THE ENGLISH BOOKS

1. *Boddhisattva and Sunyata in the Early and Developed Buddhist Traditions.*
2. *Rebirth Views in the* Śūraṅgama *Sūtra.*
3. *Commentary of Avalokiteśvara Bodhisattva.*
4. *The Key Words in Vajracchedikā Sūtra.*
5. *Sārnātha-The Cradle of Buddhism in the Archeological View.*
6. *Take Refuge in the Three Gems and Keep the Five Precepts.*
7. *Cycle of Life.*
8. *Forty Years in the Dharma: A Life of Study and Service—Venerable Bhikkhuni Giới* Hương.
9. *Sharing the Dharma -Vietnamese Buddhist Nuns in the United States.*
10. *A Buddhist Nun and American Inmates.*
11. *Daily Monastic Chanting.*
12. *Weekly Buddhist Discourse Chanting.*
13. *Practice Meditation and Pure Land.*
14. *The Ceremony for Peace.*
15. *The Lunch Offering Ritual.*
16. *The Ritual Offering Food to Hungry Ghosts.*
17. *The Pureland Course of Amitabha Sutra.*
18. *The Medicine Buddha Sutra.*

19. *The New Year Ceremony.*

20. *The Great Parinirvana Ceremony.*

21. *The Buddha's Birthday Ceremony.*

22. *The Ullambana Festival (Parents' Day).*

23. *The Marriage Ceremony.*

24. *The Blessing Ceremony for The Deceased.*

25. *The Ceremony Praising Ancestral Masters.*

26. *The Enlightened Buddha Ceremony.*

27. *The Uposatha Ceremony (Reciting Precepts).*

28. *Buddhism: A Historical and Practical Vision.* Edited by Ven. Dr. Thich Hanh Chanh and Ven. Dr. Bhikṣuṇī TN Gioi Huong.

29. *Contribution of Buddhism For World Peace & Social Harmony.* Edited by Ven. Dr. Buddha Priya Mahathero and Ven. Dr. Bhikṣuṇī TN Gioi Huong.

30. *Global Spread of Buddhism with Special Reference to Sri Lanka.* Buddhist Studies Seminar in Kandy University. Edited by Dr. Ven. Kahawatte Siri Sumedha Thero and Dr. Bhikṣuṇī TN Gioi Huong.

31. *Buddhism In Sri Lanka During The Period of 19th to 21st Centuries.* Buddhist Studies Seminar in Colombo. Edited by Prof. Ven. Medagama Nandawansa and Dr. Bhikṣuṇī TN Gioi Huong.

32. *Diary: Practicing Vipassana and the Four Foundations of Mindfulness Sutta.*

33. *Prayer for the Souls of Unborn Babies.*

34. *Nonviolent Struggle - The Foundation for Building Global Peace*

35. *History of Buddhist Education and Current Institutes of Bhikkhu, Bhikkhuni and Sīla Mātā in Sri Lanka*

1.3.THE BILINGUAL BOOKS (VIETNAMESE-ENGLISH)

1. *Bản Tin Hương Sen: Xuân, Phật* Đản, *Vu Lan (*Hương Sen Newsletter: Spring, Buddha Birthday and Vu Lan, annual/ Mỗi Năm).
2. *Danh Ngôn Nuôi Dưỡng Nhân Cách* - Good Sentences Nurture a Good Manner.
3. *Văn Hóa* Đặc *Sắc của Nước Nhật Bản*-Exploring the Unique Culture of Japan.
4. *Sống An Lạc dù* Đời *không* Đẹp *như Mơ* - Live Peacefully though Life is not Beautiful as a Dream.
5. *Hãy* Nói *Lời Yêu Thương*-Words of Love and Understanding.
6. *Văn Hóa Cổ Kim qua Hành* Hương *Chiêm* Bái -The Ancient- Present Culture in Pilgrim.
7. *Nghệ Thuật Biết Sống - Art of Living.*
8. *Dharamshala - Hành* Hương *Vùng* Đất *Thiêng, Ấn* Độ, Dharamshala - Pilgrimage to the Sacred Land, India.
9. *The Great Contribution to World Peace and Social Harmony of Emperor Ashoka and Emperor Trần Nhân Tông* - Sự *Đóng* Góp cho Hòa *Bình* Thế Giới và An Toàn Xã Hội của Hoàng *Đế* A-Dục và Vua Trần Nhân Tông.

1.4.THE TRANSLATED BOOKS

1. *Xá Lợi Của Đức Phật* (Relics of the Buddha), Tham Weng Yew.
2. *Sen Nở Nơi Chốn Tử Tù* (Lotus in Prison), many authors.
3. *Chùa Việt Nam Hải Ngoại* (Overseas Vietnamese Buddhist Temples).
4. *Việt Nam Danh Lam Cổ Tự* (The Famous Ancient Buddhist Temples in Vietnam).
5. *Hương Sen, Thơ và Nhạc* – (Lotus Fragrance, Poem and Music).
6. *Phật Giáo-Một Bậc* Đạo *Sư, Nhiều Truyền Thống* (Buddhism: One Teacher – Many Traditions), Đức Đạt Lai Lạt Ma 14th & Ni Sư Thubten Chodren.
7. *Cách Chuẩn Bị Chết và Giúp Người Sắp Chết-Quan* Điểm *Phật Giáo* (Preparing for Death and Helping the Dying – A Buddhist Perspective).

2.BUDDHIST MUSIC ALBUMS from POEMS of THÍCH NỮ GIỚI HƯƠNG

1. Đào Xuân *Lộng Ý Kinh* (The Buddha's Teachings Reflected in Cherry Flowers).
2. *Niềm Tin Tam Bảo* (Trust in the Three Gems).
3. *Trăng Tròn Nghìn Năm* Đón *Chờ Ai* (Who Is the Full Moon Waiting for for Over a Thousand Years?).
4. Ánh *Trăng Phật Pháp* (Moonlight of Dharma-Buddha).
5. *Bình Minh Tỉnh Thức* (Awakened Mind at the Dawn) (*Piano Variations for Meditation*).

6. *Tiếng Hát Già Lam* (Song from Temple).
7. *Cảnh* Đẹp *Chùa Xưa* (The Magnificent, Ancient Buddhist Temple).
8. Karaoke *Hoa* Ưu Đàm Đã *Nở* (An Udumbara Flower Is Blooming).
9. *Hương Sen Ca* (Hương Sen's Songs)
10. *Về Chùa Vui Tu* (Happily Go to Temple for Spiritual Practices)
11. *Gọi Nắng Xuân Về* (Call the Spring Sunlight).
12. Đệ *Tử Phật* (Buddhist Disciples).
13. *Hoa Pháp Cú* (Dhammapada Flower).
14. *Vu Lan B*áo Hiếu (The Filial Piety on Vu Lan Season).

Please visit: http://www.huongsentemple.com/index.php/ kinh-sach/tu-sach-bao-anh-lac

Song Ngữ Anh - Việt

THE GREAT CONTRIBUTION TO WORLD PEACE AND SOCIAL HARMONY OF EMPEROR ASHOKA AND EMPEROR TRẦN NHÂN TÔNG

SỰ ĐÓNG GÓP CHO HÒA BÌNH THẾ GIỚI VÀ AN TOÀN XÃ HỘI CỦA HOÀNG ĐẾ A-DỤC VÀ VUA TRẦN NHÂN TÔNG

Tác giả: Bảo Anh Lạc Bookshelf 101 - Thích Nữ Giới Hương

NHÀ XUẤT BẢN TÔN GIÁO

53 Tràng Thi – Hoàn Kiếm - Hà Nội

ĐT: (024)37822845

Email: nhaxuatbantongiao@gmail.com

Chịu trách nhiệm xuất bản

Giám đốc

ThS. Nguyễn Hữu Có

Chịu trách nhiệm nội dung

Tổng Biên tập

Lê Hồng Sơn

Biên tập: **Nguyễn Thị Thanh Thủy**

Trình bày và sửa bản in: **Vũ Đình Trọng**

Số lượng in: 1.000 bản, Khổ: 14 cm x 21.6 cm

In tại: Công ty T.N.HH Sản xuất Thương mại Dịch vụ In ấn Trâm Anh, 159/57 Bạch Đằng, phường 2, quận Tân Bình, Thành phố Hồ Chí Minh.

Số ĐKXB: 148-2025/CXBIPH/01-02/TG

Mã ISBN: 978-604-941-190-8

QĐXB: 98/QĐ-NXBTG ngày 21 tháng 2 năm 2025

In xong và nộp lưu chiểu năm 2025